MURRAY KORMAN

MURRAY KORMAN

THE ONE BIG NAME

CLYDE ADAMS

CLYDE ADAMS GRAPHICS • LEEDS, ALABAMA

Murray Korman: The One Big Name
by Clyde Adams

Copyright 2020. All rights reserved

Published by: Clyde Adams Graphics
220 Chimney Rock Road
Leeds, Alabama 35094
USA
murraykorman.com
clydeadams.com
clyde@clydeadams.com

All rights reserved. No part of this book may be reproduced or transmitted in any form or by any means, electronic or mechanical, including photocopying, recording or by information storage and retrieval system, without written permission from the author, except for the inclusion of brief quotations in a review.

Cover/Book Designer/Illustrator: Clyde Adams, clydeadams.com

Editors: Leslie Greaves and Judy Reveal

ISBN: 978-1-7351494-0-0

Library of Congress Control Number: 2020909695

Printed in the USA

DEDICATION

This book is dedicated
to the life and artistry
of Murray Korman.

TABLE OF CONTENTS

FOREWORD

When my mother died in 2011, I came into possession of several large boxes of negatives. They contained images taken by her uncle, Murray Korman. I knew, of course, who Murray Korman was – one of the best-known and most successful "celebrity" photographers of his day. But as I looked through the photos of Broadway and Vaudeville performers, movie stars, and New York society ladies, I came to realize what a gifted artist Murray was. It seemed a tragedy that a man of such talent should have gone down into obscurity. I wanted to do something about it, but it seemed a daunting task, and I really didn't know where to begin. I made some inquiries, but it soon came to a dead end.

Several years later I received an email from Maureen McCabe. She was writing a book about her father's Vaudeville career and wanted my consent to include a Murray Korman photo. As we corresponded, I discovered that she, too, was enamored of Murray's work. When she learned of my desire to revive my great-uncle's reputation she suggested that I contact Clyde Adams, a graphic artist in Alabama who was designing her book.

My email to Clyde received an enthusiastic response; he was as ardent an admirer of Murray Korman as I was! Clyde generously offered to digitize Murray's photos, and we set to work. I would select a few dozen negatives, do my best to identify the subjects, and ship them off to Alabama. When they were scanned and returned, I would send a few dozen more. After many months of Clyde's arduous work, the project was complete – I was elated and relieved to know that Murray's legacy, which existed so tenuously in the form of negatives, was now permanently preserved.

But Clyde was not content with being a mere archivist. He began (or, more likely, continued) his investigations into Murray Korman's life. My aunt, Roberta Satro, and I told him everything we knew about Murray; he found newspaper and magazine articles; he uncovered the most obscure records and documents; he interviewed everyone he could find who had had a personal or professional relationship with Murray.

And the result is this marvelous book, in which I have learned so much more about my great-uncle's life than I ever knew. I am ever so grateful to Clyde for writing it, and I hope that you, dear reader, will enjoy it as much as I did.

Leslie Greaves

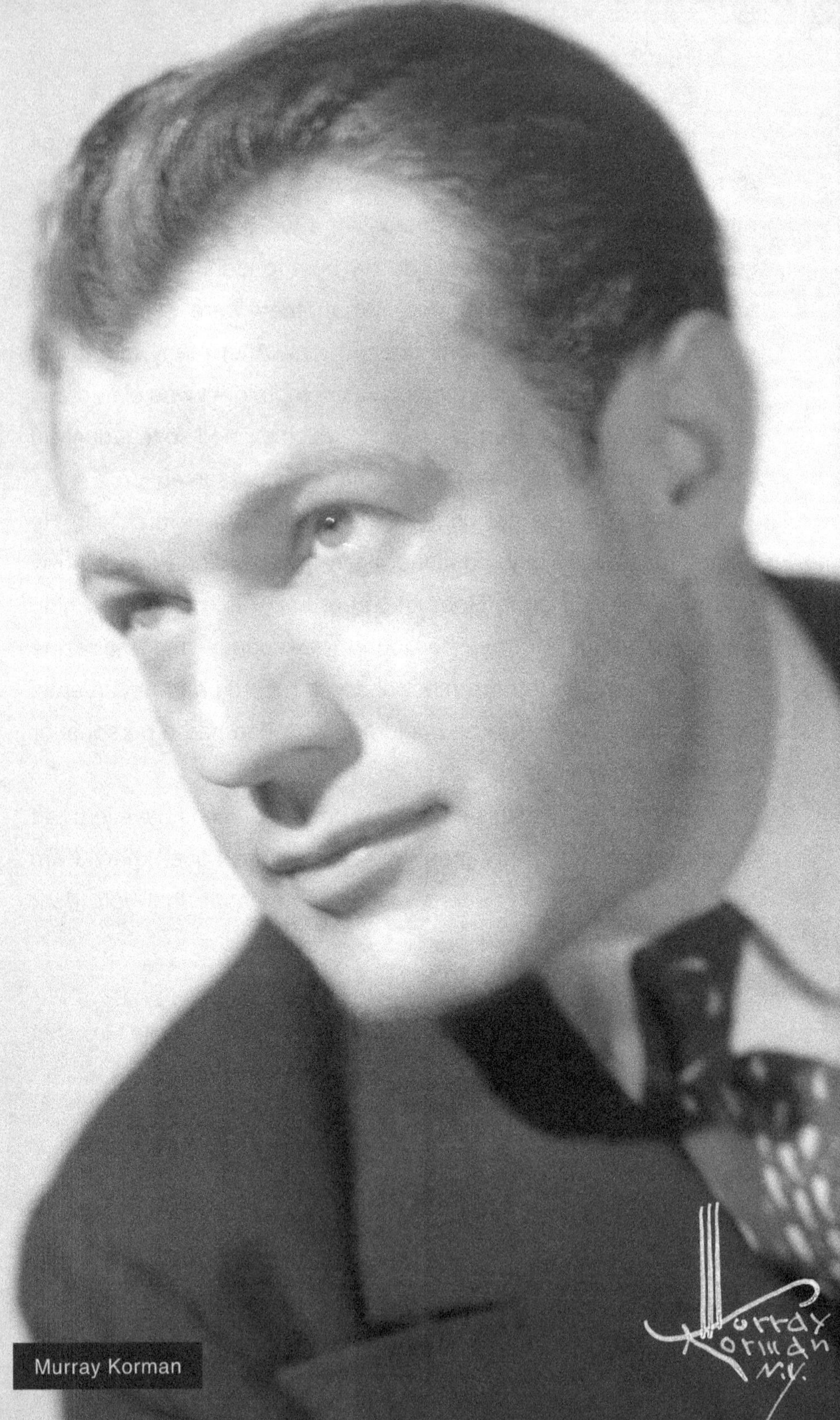

Murray Korman

PREFACE

My introduction to Murray Korman was the result of a unique set of circumstances. In 2010 I received an email from Maureen McCabe, a potential client, asking if I was interested in doing the design work for a book she was writing documenting her late father's Vaudeville career. Seems as if Weldon Barr O'Toole had a successful career on the stages of Vaudeville, which did not spark much interest in his daughter until years after he was deceased. Poring through old scrapbooks full of newspaper clippings and photos, Maureen became absorbed in her father's world. And on a tangent, she grew enamored with several striking, old publicity photos of her father that were marked with the photographer's distinct signature: Murray Korman, NY.

Maureen's curiosity, coupled with a great appreciation for the history of that era, led her, while writing and publishing the book about her father, to explore the life and works of Murray Korman. The more she discovered, the more impressed she became with him. Eventually, her hours of research led to correspondence with one of Korman's heirs; his great-niece, Leslie Greaves, an artist living in New York City. Through conversations with Leslie, Maureen discovered that Korman's meager estate was left to his two nieces, Roberta Satro and Leslie's mother, Sally Greaves. Upon Sally's death, her portion was allotted to Leslie and her sister, Melanie Baker. And, for the most part, the only items of relative value in the estate were boxes of old negatives. Immediately following Korman's death in 1961, Roberta and Sally were faced with the decision of what to do with the thousands of negatives belonging to Murray. With some haste, the sisters pored through the negatives keeping approximately six hundred, which were promptly boxed up, stored away and virtually forgotten for decades.

While working on Maureen's book I meticulously scanned and provided her with high-quality, digital files of her father's newspaper clippings and photos, taking particular pains with the Murray Korman images. Once Maureen learned of the negatives in Leslie's possession she thought of me and my scanning capabilities. Then, with a concern for their preservation, she approached me about getting involved with a potential project to scan all of the negatives. To say I was intrigued is an understatement. The idea of bringing to life images taken during this era, arguably the golden age of Broadway, and all but forgotten for at least half of a century, was a no-brainer.

Eventually, Maureen put me in touch with Leslie and a long-distance friendship began. Initially, there was some expected apprehension on Leslie's part. But once she understood my appreciation for protecting the integrity of the images and my desire to assist in resurrecting her great uncle's legacy, a partnership and friendship began. Soon packages crammed full of negatives began arriving at my doorstep. Sometimes 20 to 30, other times more, but they began arriving one bundle at a time. In my spare time, I would scan, then return the negatives and Leslie would ship another batch. With each scan, a beautiful image, hidden both in a box inside a closet as well as hidden in the hard-to-discern negative state, was brought to life.

Typically I would begin the scanning process then walk away, leaving the scanner to do it's magic while I tackled other projects. But any time the opportunity presented itself, I would sit entranced watching the image slowly come to life on my computer screen. The images alone were amazing, but the thought of being the first person in over a half-century to see the artistry of Korman unfold before my eyes was enthralling. There was a young Jackie Gleason, Eva Gabor, Gypsy Rose Lee, Bob Hope and an entire list of who's who from the world of mid-twentieth-century entertainment. For about a year, the process repeated itself; Leslie would mail negatives, I'd scan and return. Eventually, the entire collection of approximately 600 negatives were scanned, cataloged, and captured in high-resolution, digital format.

It was inevitable that early in the scanning process, like Maureen, my curiosity was piqued about the man behind the images. Who was Murray Korman and what became of him? Why had his legacy all but vanished from the chronicles of photography? Or had it? I began to gather and read anything and everything about the man and his career. I learned as much as I could from Leslie and was able to have several phone conversations with Roberta Satro, Murray's niece and heir. And as is my habit, as I gathered information I wrote everything down, trying to piece together the puzzle of his life and make sense of it. The more I gathered the more intrigued I became, and was convinced that Murray's life was a made-for-Hollywood story. And it was not long before I determined to compile my research into a book. You hold the results of that decision and the hundreds of hours spent tracking down the man behind the mystery.

Though there are many pieces of the puzzle still missing, most that may never be discovered, (and many that will remain a mystery due to the author's limited resources), I have no doubt that you'll find his story equally fascinating. My hope is you'll enjoy and appreciate the artistry and life of Murray Korman: immigrant, entrepreneur, artist, photographer and arguably the most famous, unknown New York celebrity of the twentieth century.

I'm grateful to Maureen McCabe for introducing me to Murray Korman. We both share a love and fascination with this era of America's history and the art it produced. And a special thanks to Leslie Greaves for welcoming me into her great uncle's world, trusting me with her priceless inheritance and providing support and encouragement along the way.

Clyde Adams

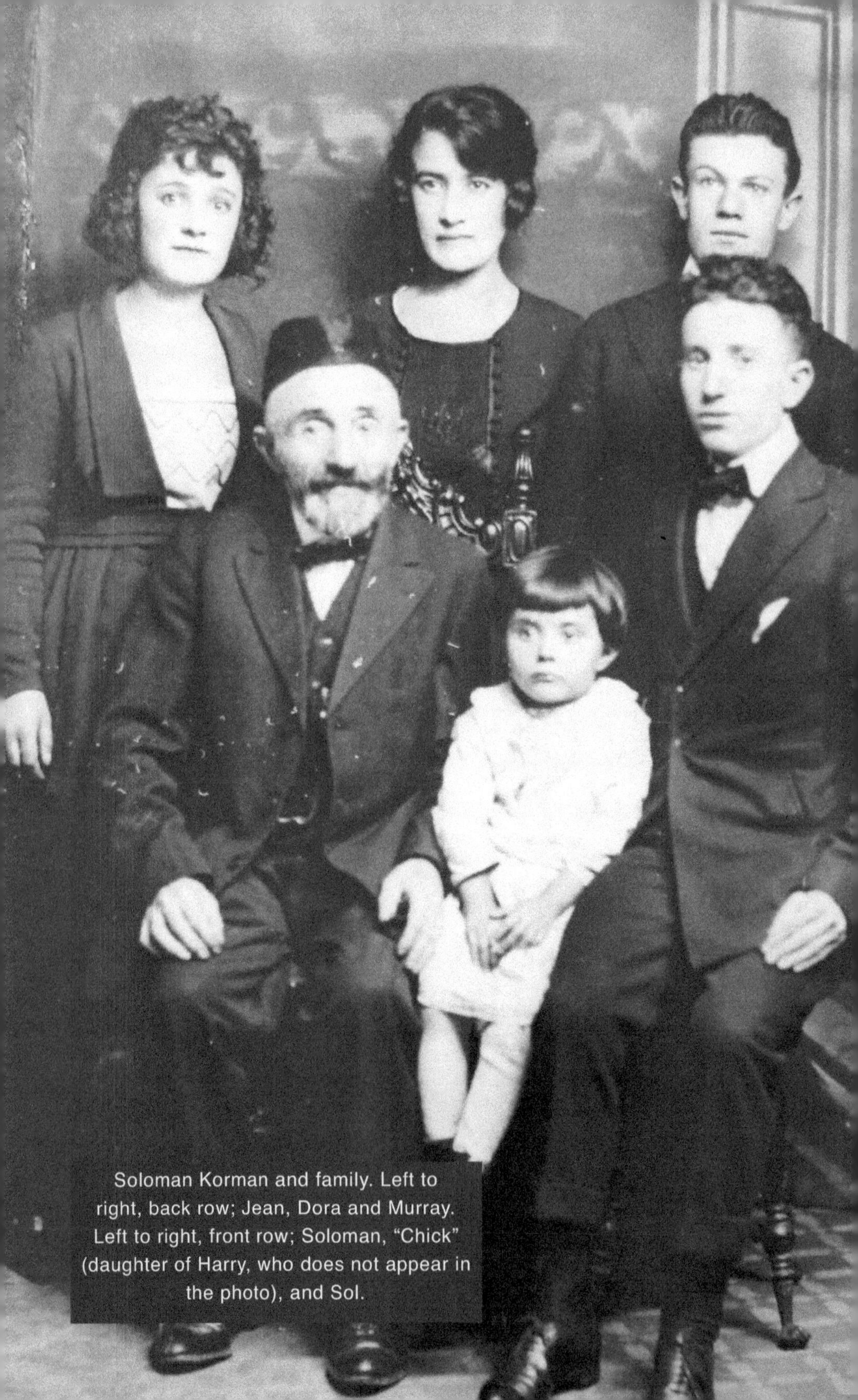

Soloman Korman and family. Left to right, back row; Jean, Dora and Murray. Left to right, front row; Soloman, “Chick” (daughter of Harry, who does not appear in the photo), and Sol.

– CHAPTER 1 –

AGAINST ALL ODDS

In contrast to his diminutive stature and defying all odds, for most of three decades, Murray Korman was a larger-than-life figure in the entertainment world and among the social elite of New York City. Short and stocky at about 5'4" and 148 pounds,[1] with hair that "eddies around his ears and down his neck, like an unemployed actor's"[2] and often referred to as disheveled, Korman earned international respect and praise for his skill with a camera. *Photo Arts Magazine,* October 1952, stated that he is "by far the most fabulous of entertainment's star-makers. Korman in the studio is a marvel to behold. No photographer, no artist, ever worked with a surer knowledge of his medium than Murray Korman, ... his name is a by-word in entertainment."

To truly appreciate his eventual rise to fame, and his accomplishments, one has to first look at the circumstances that shaped his world. To label it difficult would be a gross understatement. A feature article in *The New Yorker* magazine, October 1934, noted that "Korman...has brilliantly overcome the obstacles of a humble background."

Nineteenth-century America was a country in rapid transition. Mere decades earlier a bunch of rag-tag colonists had shocked the civilized world by going toe-to-toe with the most powerful nation on earth, finally gaining their independence from Britain. The end of that conflict was only the beginning of a long, difficult struggle to build a nation, gain economic stability, and find acceptance among other nations of the world. Few were the adventurous, brave souls who cared, or dared, to leave the comfort of their European homes and estates to seek life in this new, wild country.

But with an enviable wealth of natural resources and a self-sufficient, pioneering-spirited population, by the mid-1800s progress was significant; America was growing and standing strong. But in spite of significant gains, by all accounts the world's governmental and economic powers were still to be found in nations scattered across Europe and Asia. And then came America's Civil War, all but destroying any effort made to set America on equal ground with other nations. The very core of the union was threatened, setting America back decades in her progress.

But the end of that conflict, and the final years of the century proved to be a turning point for this fledgling democracy as the wheels of America's industrial engine began turning. By 1900 the United States had surpassed England as the leading industrial nation on earth. America's "Industrial Revolution was, and still is, the greatest engine of change in the history of humankind."[3]

Opportunities presented by this booming economy, coupled with conflicts in Europe that would eventually erupt into World War I, fueled a wave of immigrants to America's shores the likes of which the world had never seen. Promise of security and hope for a better life was the siren song that proved irresistible to a Ukranian by the name of Solomon "Sol" Korman. Following the death of his wife in 1907, and left with five young children to raise, Sol made the fateful and difficult decision to leave them behind, travel to America, and try to forge a new life for his family.

Born Moritz Korman on March 16, 1902,[a] in Kamianets-Podilskyi,[4] Ukraine,[b] Murray was the youngest of Soloman's five children; three sons and two daughters. Murray was only five years old when his mother died and his father, "who operated a small grain mill and peddled a little homemade vodka on the side,"[5] emigrated to New York City. No record exists to explain why he came alone nor who kept the five children in his absence, but it can easily be assumed that five-year-old Murray's world was turned upside down. It would be a few years later before Murray and his siblings joined their father.[c] A 1942 interview with Murray shared

a There's some discrepancy about Korman's date of birth. Most sources list 1902 as his birth year but one web site lists 1900. (http://broadway.cas.sc.edu/content/murray-korman)

b As with the date of birth, the location of Korman's birth is disputed. According to the same source in the footnote above, Korman was born in the city of Podolsk, Russia. However Wikipedia and Everipedia list Kamenets Podolsk, Podolia, Russian Empire as his place of birth. The city of Podolsk is located just south of Moscow whereas Kamianets-Podilskyi is a city in western Ukraine. At the time of Korman's birth Kamianets-Podilskyi, Ukraine, was part of the Russian Empire.

c Sources are contradictory as to when Murray Korman and his siblings came to America. One source records 1907 as the year Korman immigrated, the same year as his father, while another reads "Korman and his parents emigrated in 1912". Still, a third source notes that the five children followed their father "a few years later." Though not an exact date, this last time frame seems most reliable and corresponds with the information the author received during a 2013 interview with Roberta Satro, a niece of Korman and heir to his estate. When asked, Roberta said "the children followed several years after their father." Roberta also verified that Korman's mother died prior to the family emigrating, contradictory to the source that alludes to them immigrating together.

insight that raises more questions about the circumstances of his immigration: "We were smuggled out, political reasons. Something about selling liquor."[6]

Soon after being reunited, the Kormans settled on Ludlow Street in New York City's Lower East Side neighborhood in the borough of Manhattan, joining a great wave of Jewish immigrants from Russia, Poland, and Eastern Europe that had begun in the 1880s. According to one source, by 1894 the population in the Lower East Side "reached an astonishing 986 people per acre—one-and-a-half times that of Bombay, India!"[7] This influx continued until approximately 1920, creating the backdrop for Korman's life. And so it was within a few short years that Murray was transported from a childhood hometown with a population of approximately 40,000,[a] to one of the largest metropolitan areas in the world.

Sol Korman brought into this melting pot a penchant for self-employment that not only sustained him and his young family but allowed them to prosper. For several years he worked at seasonal occupations such as vending fruit in the summer and shoveling snow in the winter. Then, undoubtedly taking advantage of the great human resources around him, Sol began a small but successful garment manufacturing business. Though there are no records to verify it, surely Sol's children were "employed" in his business in some capacity. And just as certainly, a young Murray was influenced by his father's entrepreneurial spirit.

a According to the Russian census of 1897, Kamianets-Podilskyi had a population of 35,934.

The Korman children were enrolled in school and Murray found himself in New York City's Public School 13, then later Public School 160. And as with most of his early childhood, some clear assumptions can be made. Regarding his entry into the American public school system, surely he struggled to learn the language. At this time in history, English was not as universally accepted and taught as it is in the 21st century so it's doubtful Murray was taught English before coming to America. This, and the difficulties it represents, could very well be a major factor in his early exit from public school and his less than favorable opinion of school.

But it was during his time in public school that Korman's creative bent and love of art was first documented. During the brief period he attended public school in America one former teacher noted that he "drew caricatures of the teachers and made a general nuisance of himself." "All I wanted to do was make pictures. I enjoyed school. They had free chalk," Korman admitted.[8]

But Korman's apparent carefree approach to school was in stark contrast to his work ethic and drive to succeed, very likely modeled after his father's. Murray took full advantage of the opportunities America offered. As a youth, he sold newspapers, designed rugs, and painted dolls. It's this third occupation that proved most rewarding, jump-starting a successful career in the creative arts and photography.

It was 1909 when Rose O'Neill's Cupid-like Kewpie doll character first came on the scene as an illustration for *Ladies Home*

Journal.[9] Its subsequent popularity resulted in Kewpie Kutouts, the first two-sided paper dolls printed in *Woman's Home Companion* in 1912. That same year, a New York distributor of dolls, toys, and novelty items, George Borgfeldt & Company, approached O'Neill about developing a line of original Kewpie dolls and figurines and offered to "help her keep up with the overwhelming demand for Kewpie merchandise."[10] A 17-year-old art student, Joseph Kallus, was hired to create the first models and molds of Kewpie dolls and novelty items, which were then mass-produced in Germany. These, too, were an immediate hit. But the onset of WWI brought an end to doll production at the German factories. In response to this setback, Joseph Kallus founded the Rex Doll Company and began the production of dolls in New York City in 1916.

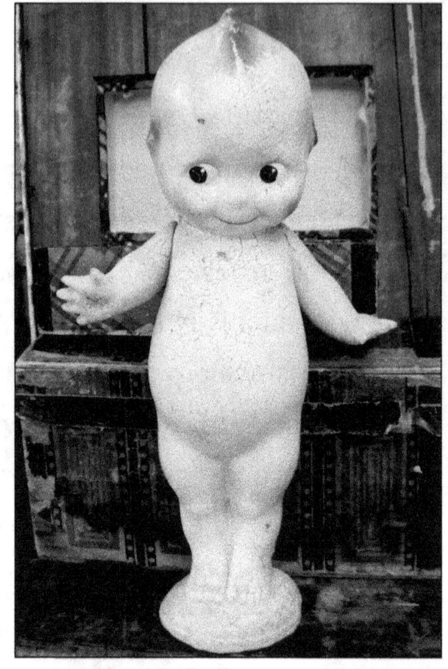

Kewpie Doll, circa 1921

This was the first of many unique, almost providential, sets of circumstances that afforded Murray Korman the chance to achieve his American dream. It was as if around every corner opportunity would knock, and Murray entered without hesitation. The same year that the Rex Doll Company opened its doors, Korman, only 14 years old and in the eighth grade, landed a part-time job with the company, painting faces on Kewpie dolls. He excelled at this craft and was soon offered $50 a week to work full-time, an offer too good to refuse. And so he dropped out of school during his eighth-grade year, to pursue full-time employment.

He soon proved to be gifted with management skills that matched his artistic talents. Within a short time, Korman had 20 "daubers" working under him.[11] But his good fortune did not stop there. Due to his "brisk efficiency and all-around skill, the factory decided to let out all the painting to him on a contract basis, and he set up his own shop."[12]

In 1919,[a] Korman decided to further his artistic career and enrolled in night classes at Cooper Union to study art, something he continued for three years.[13] As was the pattern for most of his life, he excelled and after his first year of "freehand" was promoted to "third year."[14] He also began to land some freelance jobs sketching illustrations for local newspapers, all the while continuing to paint Kewpies.

Fresh out of Cooper Union in 1922, Korman landed a job as a sketch artist for the New York publication *Morning Telegraph*. While there, "one of his pet jobs was to cover the theatre openings with his facile pencil and sketch-pad." (This was during an era when staff sketch artists were the equivalent of today's staff photographers.) Already enchanted by the world of entertainment, this job fueled his

a The date of 1919 appears in Christine Trotter's on-line article and differs from the date of 1917 given in *The New Yorker* magazine article listed in the endnotes. According to Trotter's reference, Ellen Dorsey (Associate Registrar, Office of Admissions and Records at the Cooper Union), Korman began his studies at Cooper Union in 1919 (age 16). "After his first year of 'freehand,' he was promoted to third year. Institutional records show he attended until 1921. Their records list his occupation as 'painter.'"

aspirations to become a leading "publisher" of its legion of beautiful women.[15]

Finally in 1924, though making a handsome sum of $300 per week, he quit the doll painting business to pursue a full-time career as a sketch artist and painter.[16/17] As one journalist said, "he left dolls in favor of the more exciting but less remunerative profession of newspaper illustration of, as one might suspect, beautiful women in New York."[18]

In 1928, the same year Korman submitted his petition for naturalization, he was working as a sketch artist for a Spanish language newspaper, *La Prensa.* And his short-lived comic strip, "Poor Paddy" was appearing in some New England papers.[19]

Korman's next opportunity came from the *New York World*[a] newspaper (a local paper with a 1931 circulation of 313,000) with Broadway as his specific assignment.[20] His artistic talent had also captured the attention of Emile Gauvreau, a local newspaper editor who gave him several freelance assignments for his publication, *The New York Graphic.*

Prompted by these continued successes, Korman opened a portrait studio. The studio's first high-profile job, and at the time, Korman's most significant, came when Florenz Ziegfeld commissioned a large sketch of the entire Ziegfeld Follies cast for publicity purposes. For this, he was paid the handsome sum

a The *Popular Photography* article dated November, 1937, is quoted as saying "fresh from an art course at Cooper Union, he was a staff cartoonist for the sporty and horsey *Morning Telegraph.*" This contradicts a separate article that ran in publications across the nation in the latter part of December, 1938, that says Korman's "artistic life" began as a "cartoonist" for the *New York World* newspaper. Considering that Korman began at Cooper Union in 1919 and spent 3 years there, the *Popular Photography* article insinuates that somewhere around 1922 Korman began work for *Morning Telegraph.* The author assumes that since Korman confessed to a short tenure at the *Morning Telegraph*, and an allure of all things Broadway, and his stint with the *New York World* had a specific Broadway assignment, then Korman most likely got his start at the *Morning Telegraph* followed by the *New York World* job.

of $300 and the door to artistic success was opened wide.[21] Soon other theaters were knocking on his door requesting publicity sketches of their stars. He also found himself doing personal portraits for celebrities as well as clients in the music business wanting portraits for the covers of their sheet music. There were even requests for magazine illustrations, most notably one for Edgar Allan Poe's *The Balloon Hoax,* published in the August 1927 issue of *Aviation Stories and Mechanics* magazine.

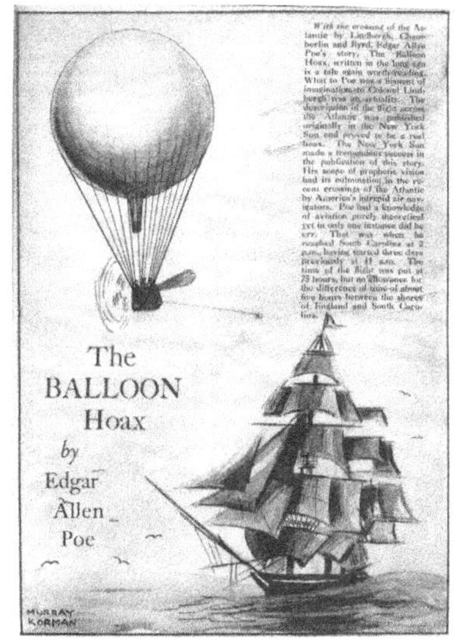

The Balloon Hoax illustration by Korman

By now the allure of Broadway held him captive, particularly the beautiful stars of the theater stages. As Korman simply stated, "Theatre fascinated [me] more than newspaper work."[22]

It was early 1906 when the headlines of *The World Magazine* cover read "12 New Americans a Minute." That's the equivalent of over six million immigrants annually competing for the American dream. It was at about this same time Korman began his quest for that dream. Though still very early in his career, Korman had already defied the odds. Surely for every person who attained even a modicum of success, hundreds fell short. But Murray had found success— and he had only just begun.

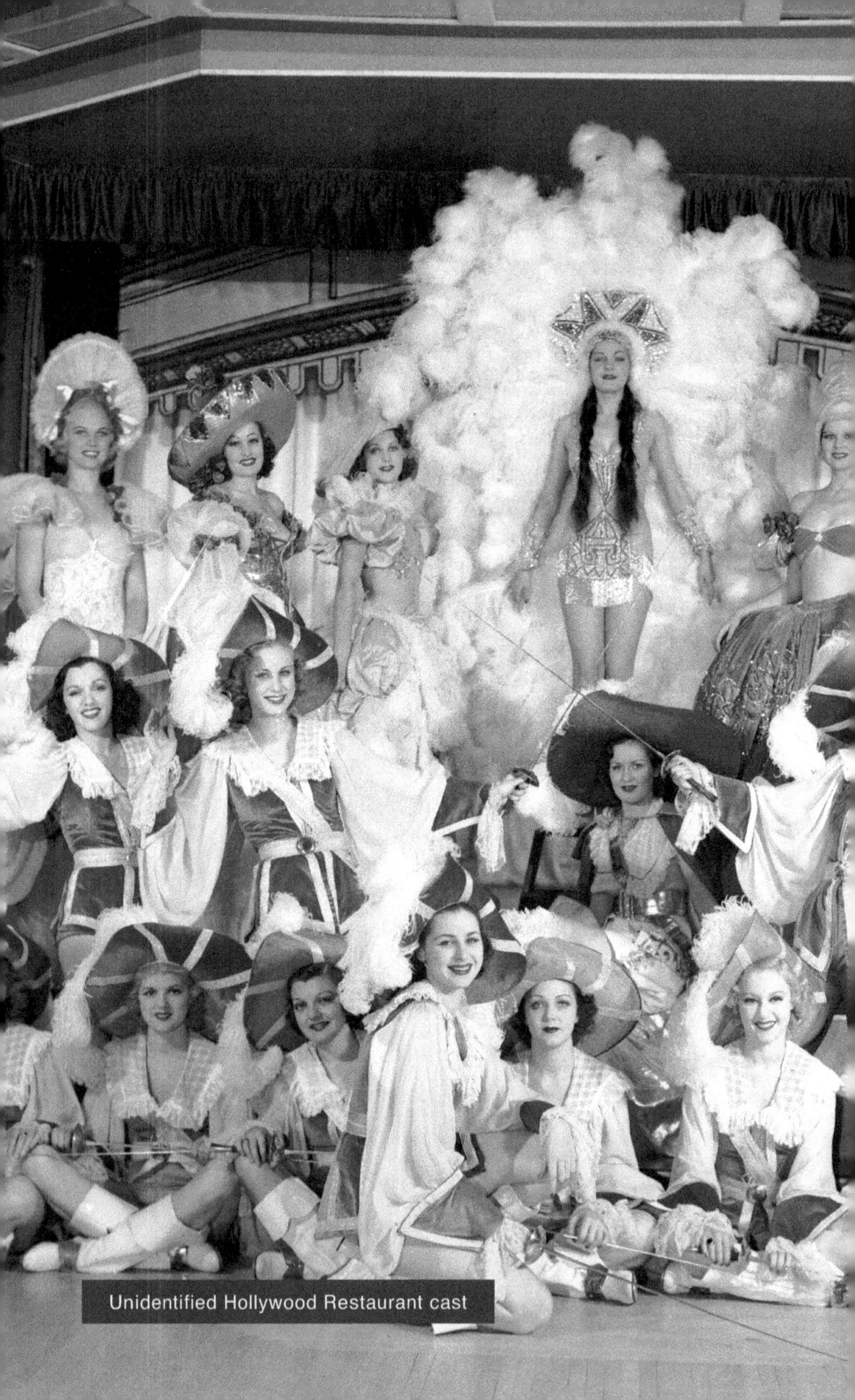

Unidentified Hollywood Restaurant cast

– CHAPTER 2 –

BROADWAY'S ALLURE

The word Broadway has long been synonymous with theatrical entertainment. Specifically, Broadway refers to the world's largest collection of live theater stages, located in the area from West 41st to West 54th Streets and 6th to 8th Avenues in New York City.[23]

The first New York theater opened in 1750, but in 1775 the Revolutionary War suspended most forms of large-scale entertainment and Broadway fell silent. Then, in 1798, theater returned in a grand way with the opening of the 2000-seat Park Theatre on Chatham Street (now Park Row).[24] It was followed by the opening of the Bowery Theater in 1826 and the 3000-seat Niblo's Garden in 1829. And so for the remainder of the 19th century, the New York theater scene exploded.

But it was not until the end of the 19th century and the early years of the 20th century that Broadway found its lights. Literally. "The world's first electrically-lit large commercial billboard was erected over Madison Square in 1892"[25] and the first electric marquees first appeared in 1906. Colored bulbs were initially used but quickly gave way to white lights because they lasted significantly longer. Electric streetlights replaced gas versions and, combined with ever more elaborate marquees, "soon [Broadway] became known throughout the world as the Great White Way,"[26] a term first coined in the February 3, 1902, edition of the *New York Evening Telegram.*[27]

In 1927, the journalist Will Irwin vividly captured the district's look and energy: "Mildly insane by day, the square goes divinely mad by night. For then on every wall, above every cornice, in every nook and cranny, blossom and dance the electric advertising signs ... All other American cities imitate them, but none gets this massed effect of tremendous jazz interpreted in light."[28]

This is the world that a young Korman found himself in. The bright lights and beautiful people were intoxicating, especially in light of his early successes. This environment, coupled with his charismatic personality, artistic talent, and entrepreneurial spirit, proved to be his formula for fame and fortune.

It can be argued that the early 20th century was Broadway's heyday; the time frame that found Murray Korman at its center. His fame was on the rise as requests for sketches from the Broadway crowd were pouring in. And though his financial intake was very comfortable, he recognized that compared to its potential it was relatively small.[29] An initial attempt to rectify this was to sell his original sketches, that were created for newspapers, to the subjects themselves. A second step was one that would change the course of his life forever. During his time working "for the *New York World*, he found it expedient to take photos of subjects then work on sketches at his leisure in the office."[30] Everything about Broadway moved at a hectic pace and Korman soon reasoned that this new approach was by far the best way to keep up with, or surpass, demand, which in turn would increase income. And so it was that Korman's initial foray into the world of photography was not necessarily due to a desire to change his artistic medium. It was born more out of the necessity of keeping pace with the demand for sketches as well as the allure of greater financial gain.

It was 1926 when he began to take full advantage of this process and the trajectory of his career, and his professional life took a dramatic upward turn. That year he approached a local photographer who was "having a tough time getting by" and offered to double his business in two weeks.[31] Korman proposed to combine his Broadway connections with the photographer's skills. Agreements were reached and a partnership was soon formed. Korman continued sketching and working from photos taken by his newfound partner and quickly found that what normally took days, could now be accomplished in mere hours. Ever the entrepreneur, Korman also discovered that money could be made by photographing the original sketches and selling these photographic prints to the performers who needed them for professional purposes.

This partnership not only allowed Korman to expand his business and pad his bank account, but it also provided

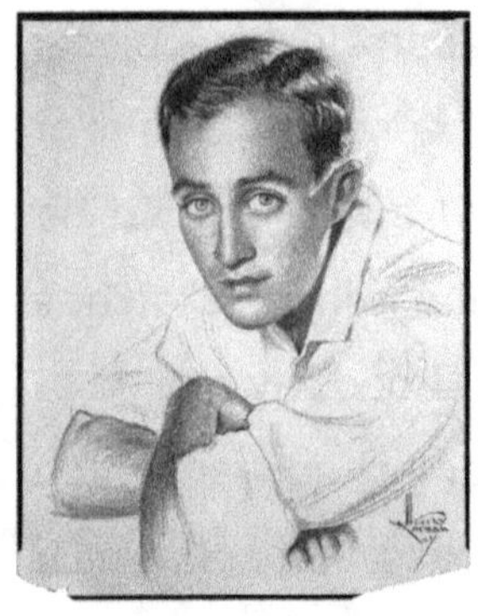
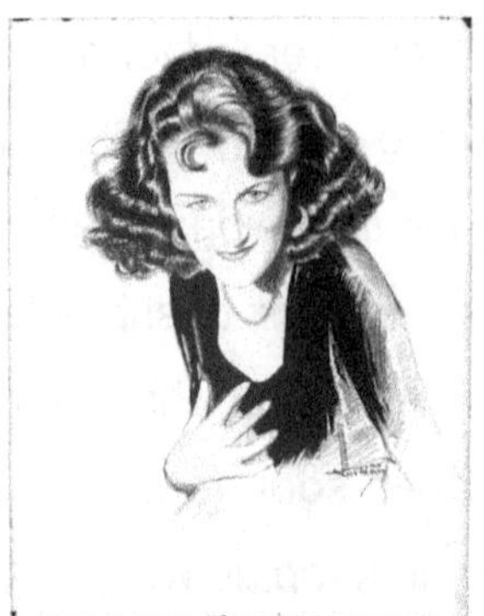
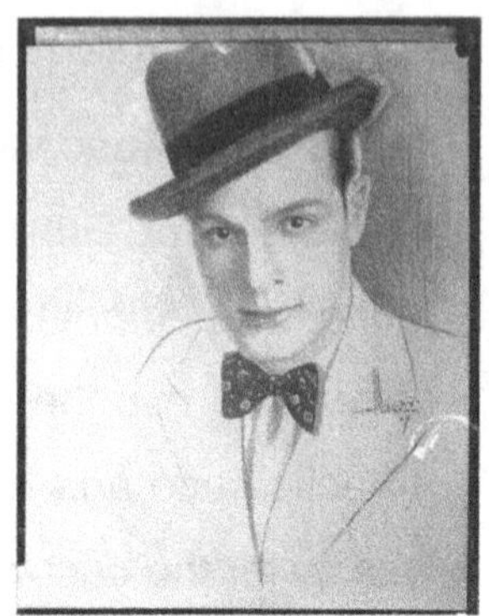

Examples of Korman's portrait sketches

the opportunity to gain a working knowledge of the basics of photography. Within a mere six months, he had acquired enough knowledge of the techniques necessary with the camera to open a photography studio of his own at 41 West 46th Street. Though a talented sketch artist, Korman soon concluded that, "in most cases, the photographs were far superior to the resulting sketches."[32] The natural progression would be to abandon sketching altogether and simply photograph the subjects. But Korman's sketches were still in demand. As late as August of 1929 producer Bernard Levey hired Korman to provide promotional sketches of his leading players and sketches for all his lobby displays. This job was for a series of six plays he was to produce, a very significant amount of work.[33] And that same year Korman's most lucrative offer to date came his way. He was offered $2500 (the equivalent of almost $37,000 in 2020) to draw a portrait of Barclay H. Warburton, Jr.[34]

But Korman soon discovered that same amount of time spent satisfactorily completing one drawing – 8 to 10 hours – was now spent producing 40 photographs[35] and the emphasis of his business

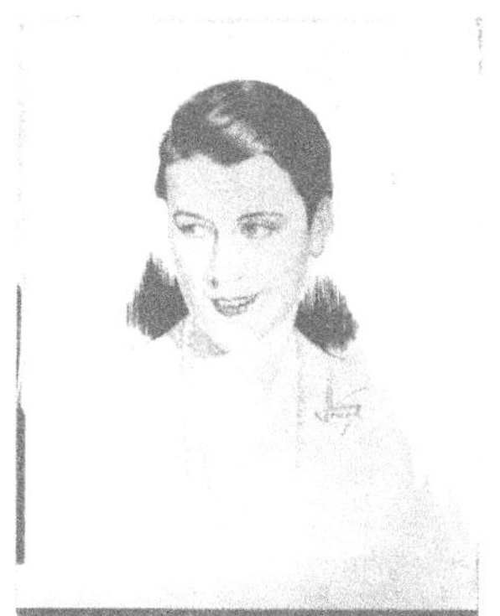 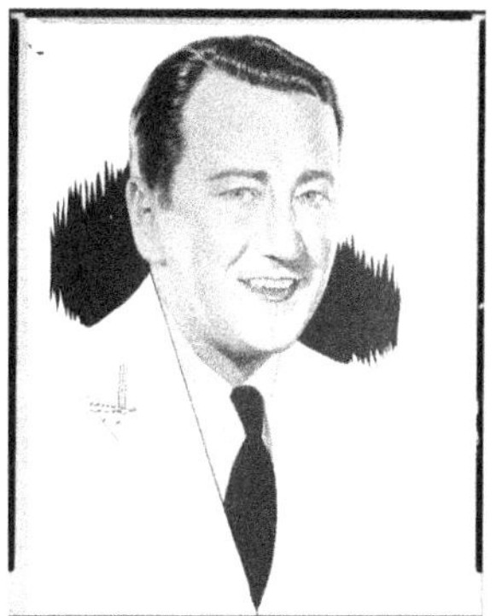 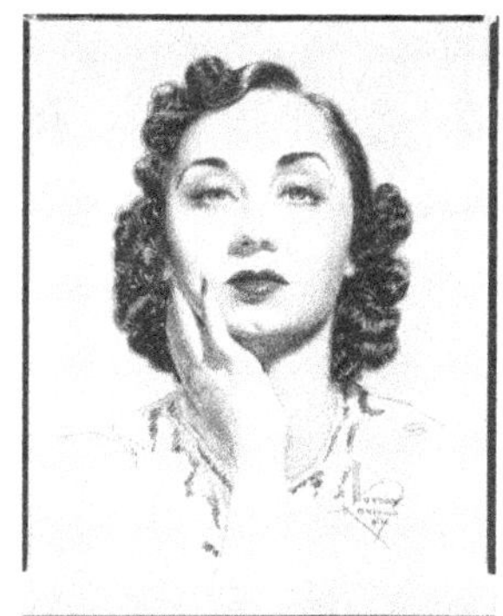

inevitably turned from sketches to photos — and successes were immediate. So it was with a certain degree of reluctance that Korman made this move away from pad and pencil. "Michelangelo would of done the same," he said.[36]

Lucrative, large sketch jobs were relatively common at this point in Korman's career. But his first significant project as a photographer came from New York City's Hollywood Restaurant. "The first big job I ever did was on the Hollywood Restaurant. The shots of the women were so appealing that someone stole them all the first night they were displayed," Korman said.[37] In the latter months of 1929, when many other photographers were closing shop, Korman was handling all lobby displays for the Palace Theatre where he had his own office on-site, and still rented a larger place on the fifth floor of a building at 701 Seventh Avenue.[38] It's a testament to his talent and business acumen that the 1930s, the heart of the longest, deepest, and most widespread depression

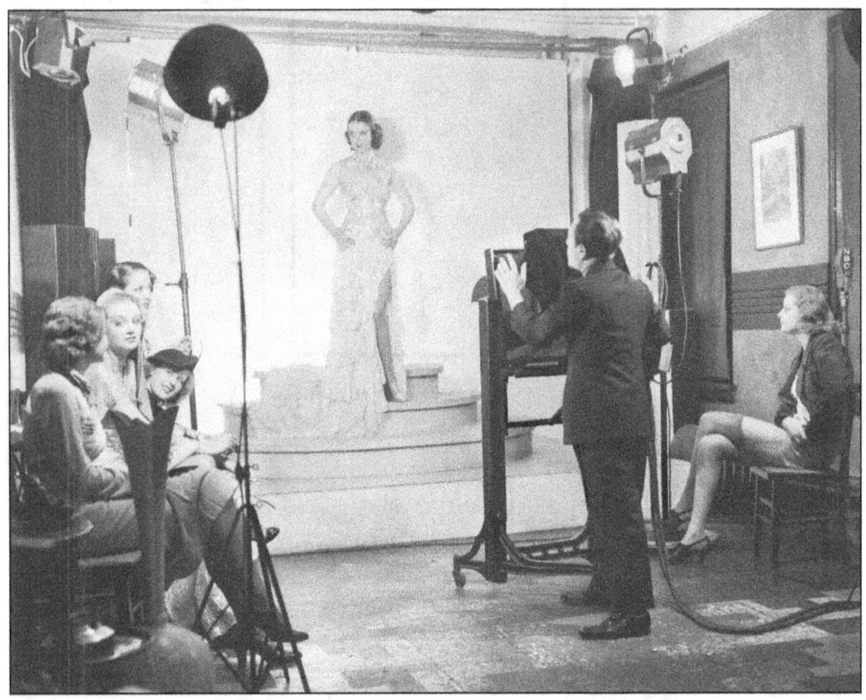

Korman in his studio with unidentified clients

of the 20th century, saw Korman's fortunes skyrocket. In October 1933, columnist James Aswell wrote: "If a delectable young lady of the ensemble wishes a picture of herself for the foyer, without too much clothing between herself and the lens, she will probably go to Murray Korman, a young man who has made quite a reputation for himself in the pleasant work." He further commented that "Professor Korman, a high-minded young man, who talks of Art and Beauty, [...is] a spectacular magician with the lens and lights."[39]

Korman's business thrived as he became a master of "cheesecake" photography, a style that "conspicuously emphasizes a woman's femininity."[40] And it was only a matter of a few years before an article by Robert Lewis Taylor, entitled *The Pleasant Art of Cheesecake,* in *The New Yorker* magazine referred to Korman's business as "probably Broadway's most successful studio."[41] His studio, that started in a small room in a hotel, soon filled three floors of the Mayfair Theatre building.[42] A 1938 article stated that "Mr. Korman has a one-man monopoly."[43] Taylor's article boldly concluded that "Korman has no peer."

At the height of his career, to enter the world of Murray Korman one had only to venture a block off-Broadway, to the aforementioned Mayfair Theatre Building, on the corner of Seventh Avenue and 47th Street.[a] This location placed him a short walk from virtually every theatre, dance hall, night club and burlesque house in the district. Entering the ground floor of the 10-story building, you'd make your way across the dim-lit lobby to a small elevator, operated by a hearty gentleman who inadvertently stops at floors along the way to your fifth-floor destination. Stepping out of the elevator you were greeted by a photographic montage of beautiful women as well as a waiting room filled with chorus girls, models, actresses, and other would-be theatrical aspirants. You're soon greeted by his "popular secretary Betty, a brunette of striking beauty."[44] If you arrive before 10:00 a.m. chances are you'll not see Korman. As was his habit, Murray typically lingered too long at Lindy's, his favorite breakfast spot, where he "was continually crying out greetings to friends between swallows of ham and eggs and French fried potatoes and

a This particular location was mentioned in an article in the *Arizona Republic,* dated June, 1941. It corresponds to *The New Yorker* article of October, 1942, which mentions the location as "..on the fifth floor of a building at 701 Seventh Avenue." But in January, 1944, a Private John Young wrote to the *Honolulu Advertiser* requesting the address of Korman's studio. The Q&A column noted that "[Korman has] three locations in New York City. They are: 675 Fifth Ave.,. 534 Madison Ave., and 701 Seventh Ave."

rolls."[45] Journalist John Ferris commented that Korman "invariably arrives in the late afternoon, but everybody in the place seems to entertain a curious notion that he'll be early."[46]

The office, at its peak, employed about 12 individuals. Typically, there were two receptionists, two secretaries, three sales representatives, two retouchers, a file clerk, two assistant photographers, and an office boy.[47] Among the employees are several family members. For most of his career, Murray's brother, Harry handled the theatrical and financial side of the business.[48] And for a while, Murray's brother, Sol, an aspiring photographer himself, assisted in the studios.

Eventually, Korman shuffles briskly through the door, typically long after his first scheduled appointments, and greets everyone with "morning, kids" though it's early afternoon. With few pleasantries to offer, Korman dashes down a long corridor to the studio. This room, long, narrow and cluttered, is where Korman is truly in his element. To one side is a curtained doorway that leads to a tiny dressing room, holding as many as four girls preparing for their time in front of Murray's lens. Dashing in and out of the room, with a great deal of shouting, mugging, and wise-cracking, Murray studies his next sitter, offers advice, orders the right lighting, then finally assumes his place behind the camera. One journalist noted that the scene at his Broadway studio was "something out of a Hollywood script – prop and klieg lights[a] in wild disarray, beautiful women thronging the waiting rooms from 10 a.m. until midnight, and the maestro dashing from one studio to another."[49]

---

a Named after the German-born American brothers who invented it, John and Anton Kliegl, a klieg light is an intense carbon arc lamp used almost exclusively in photography and filmmaking.

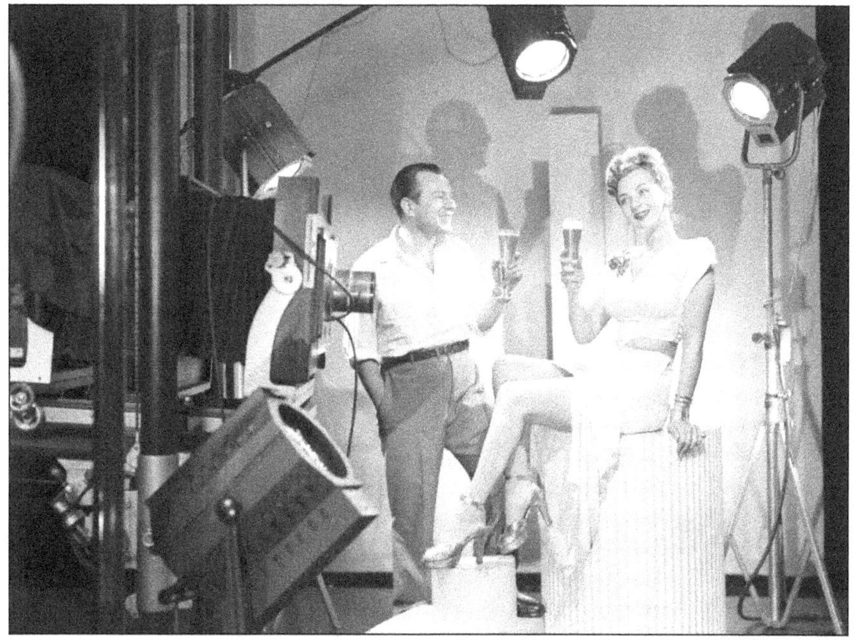

Korman shooting an ad for Piels Beer with unidentified model

It's then, behind the camera and under the hood, that the master takes full control. Though often described as amiable, by all accounts Korman was a commanding, if not demanding, presence in his studio. He worked at a furious pace, shouting commands to an array of assistants and addressing his clients in "sharp, terse sentences, yet his personal manner [was always] charming." A *Popular Photography* article noted that "If you have known Korman but a few minutes, you can readily understand why the girls have so much confidence in him. His is a vital and commanding personality and he'll ask a woman to pose this way or that in such a severe and impersonal tone that there is no question of her not doing it."[50] It's this pace that, during Korman's studios' heyday, produced 10,000 prints a week.[51]

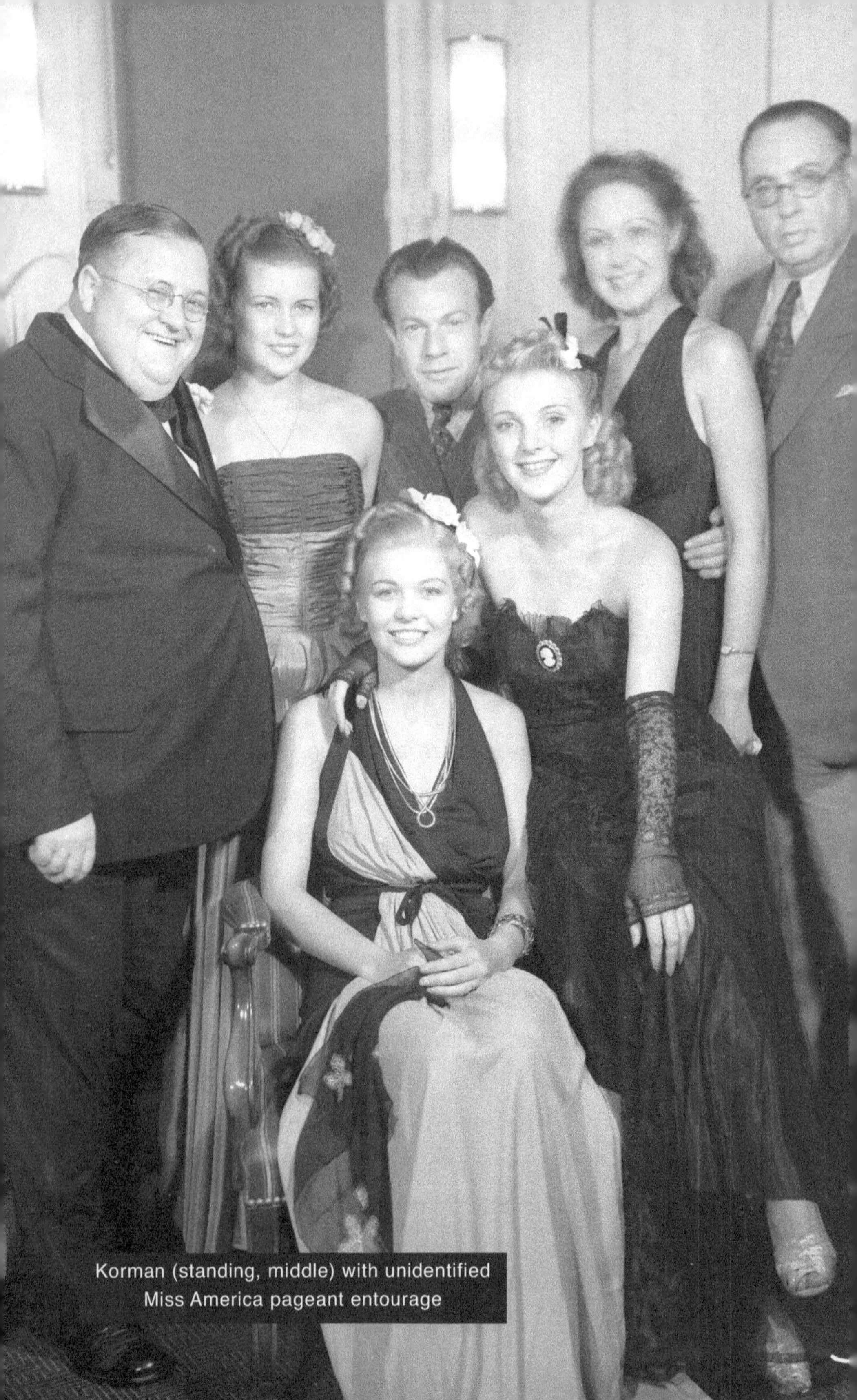

Korman (standing, middle) with unidentified
Miss America pageant entourage

– CHAPTER 3 –

MADISON AVENUE

Though Broadway was responsible for the siren call that lured him into photography, the day came when Korman determined his artistry could serve another clientele with equal success. With his usual bravado, he is quoted as saying "I kept seeing these people in the papers, and they looked pitiful. I decided to do something for them."[52]

These pitiful looking people Korman was talking about were members of what was then referred to as the "carriage trade" or "cafe society."[a] Though certainly a kind gesture, as with any successful business owner, Murray's greater interest was in the advancement of Korman Photography, and in turn, Murray himself.

And so it was that Murray made headlines in 1938 with the opening of a second location on the second floor of a quiet building at 534 Madison Avenue.[53] This swank, East Side location was the result of Korman's confidence that he could improve on New York's

a Webster defines carriage trade as "trade from well-to-do or upper-class people" and cafe society as "society of persons who are regular patrons of fashionable cafés."

cafe society portraiture that was appearing in local papers. And his impact was felt immediately in the New York City photography scene. According to one publication, "Society photographers are a little concerned about the inroads [Korman] is making on their business. Many cafe society buds, it seems, prefer the glittering products of the Korman mill to the more dignified 'portraits' which convention used to dictate."[54]

These clients were wealthy business owners who simply wanted a more flattering photo hanging in their living room or office, wives of the wealthy drawn by a desire to mimic the glamour of Broadway stars, Miss America winners, and many others who admired Korman's work but considered themselves too dignified to venture into his Broadway studio. Names like Rockefeller, Hammerstein, Manville, and Rubinstein became clients. But it's most likely that the most famous personality of that time to visit the new studio was author, politician, and eventual U.S. Ambassador Clare Boothe Luce, and Korman was completely unaware.

Born Ann Clare Boothe in New York City in 1903, Luce had a very brief Broadway career as a child. Following her ambitious mother's plan for her to become an actress, she landed her one and only role on Broadway at the age of 11. Eventually, her fertile imagination and sharp wit lead her to become a successful playwright in the early 1930s as well as a caption writer at *Vogue* and then, associate editor and managing editor of *Vanity Fair.*[55] In 1935 she married Henry Luce, the publisher of *Time*, *Life*, and

Fortune. After German and Japanese hostilities initiated WWII, but prior to America's entry into the conflicts, Luce became a war journalist traveling to war zones across the world. Then in 1942 she tossed her hat into the political arena and won a Republican seat in the United States House of Representatives representing Fairfield County, Connecticut.

The exact date of her encounter with Korman is not certain but was recorded in the October 3, 1942 issue of *The New Yorker* by writer Robert Lewis Taylor. As was common, a magazine editor contacted the studio one day to set up an appointment for a photoshoot but didn't give the subject's name. Korman assumed the editor had noticed something special in a model, as he was told "We want you to give her the glamorous treatment." The editor along with the lady showed up a bit later and Murray began his work. As he was finishing up, he offered the young lady an opportunity to make a few extra dollars by coming back around and posing for "corset and girdle work." She politely turned down the offer. The next month, when Murray picked up a copy of *Vogue* and saw his artistry, and the lady was identified as Clare Luce, "I called up the editor and raised hell" Korman said. To which the editor replied, 'Don't worry about it. It's quite all right. Mrs. Luce was never more flattered.'"[56]

There was little doubt that Korman was off and running with his Madison Avenue studio, but within this segment of society, it was the world of the New York City debutantes that seem to have taken the greatest interest in his work. Brenda Frazier, considered by many to be the face of the New York debutantes, became a client and was occasionally seen in public with Murray. Common were full-page newspaper spreads filled with photos from Korman Photography of the latest debutantes and would-be debutantes. Publications even went so far as to request Murray's opinion about debutantes and their social activities, viewing him as an expert on the subject. A prominent article in the January 12, 1941 edition of the *Philadelphia Inquirer* featured an interview with Korman, seeking his opinion of who might win the upcoming New York debutante competition. Of course, he gladly gave it: "It will be tall, brown-haired Hope Carroll. She is more than what we term photogenic. Of course, her features are perfect, her figure gracefully slender. But she has vibrancy, winsomeness, gaiety and a wholesome youthfulness very appealing to the photographer."

Recognizing and adapting to the vast differences among his clientele was a large part of Korman's genius. From its very inception, he applied this approach at his Madison Avenue studio. Doubtless, his expertise behind the camera as well as his distinct style was fundamental to his professional achievements. But the virtual overnight success of the new studio can be largely attributed to the fact that while his Broadway studio was chaotic, disheveled, and frenzied, the Madison Avenue studio was relaxed and sophisticated. Though separated by less than a mile, the two studios were worlds apart in regard to their atmosphere and the style in which they were managed, and the difference was evident even before one entered the building. Whereas the Broadway location was most noticeable by the pineapple juice stand just outside its front door,[57] the Madison Avenue studio was situated among expensive, upscale shops. And the sidewalk view was only the beginning of the grander experience clients could expect. Once in the building they would proceed up thickly carpeted stairs to the second-floor studio where walls were lined with framed portraits of debutantes. A larger, more prominent portrait was elegantly featured on a decorative easel beside the lobby's marble fireplace. Flowers adorned the window sills that flanked the receptionist whose voice sounded as if she may have had speech training.[58]

And not only was the studio's atmosphere different, but Korman himself took on a unique persona every time he entered the East Side studio. For starters, instead of rolled-up shirt sleeves, he put on a more dignified smock. And in sharp contrast to the Broadway studio, his manner was described as quiet, speaking in "modulated tones," giving advice and talking about glamour.[59] Robert Lewis Taylor in his *The New Yorker* article said of Korman in his Madison Avenue location: "He is courtly but firm; he speaks the language of his high-born customers expertly but with imperiousness."

Taylor gives the following detailed account of Korman's interaction with one of his cafe-society clients, Mrs. Forbes.

> [Leaving the Broadway studio, Korman] gathered up his hat, coat, and tie, took a taxi across town and rushed upstairs to the studio. He went in by a back entrance and put on a baggy blue smock and a beret that

he keeps on hand for important jobs. Then he went into the waiting room. Extending his left hand gracefully, he said "Mrs. Forbes, how nice." He turned to his receptionist and said, "Doesn't Mrs. Forbe's hair look lovely? Such a lovely texture." Then, "Mrs. Forbes, shall we enter?" They swept into the studio, Korman leading the way. He next escorted her to the dressing room. "I want to give just the tiniest touch to your makeup," he said. "You don't need much enhancements, Mrs. Forbes. Nature has done her work well." Then he applied a darker powder to her face, penciled her eyebrows, combed her hair, and reshaped her mouth with a different shade of lipstick. When these operations were finished, he stepped back and cried, "How refreshing! *Allons*, Mrs. Forbes!" Korman led her to a chair on the platform and went to the camera, crying out on the way, "Lights!" There was nobody else in the studio, his assistants being on Broadway at the moment, so he turned on the lights himself. Then he leaned over and squinted through the camera. "Mrs. Forbes," he called, "look up! Look at the chandelier. It's a man. You love him. He's just come into your life. Mouth a little open. The eyes wide, like Loretta Young...A little more with the mouth...Good. Now let's see the teeth... Ah, that's fine. No, not so much of a smile. This is a child's expression, bewildered, adoring. Turn the head a little. Up, up, up! Hold it...Mrs. Forbes," he said softly, walking up to her rapidly and taking both of her hands, "it was enchanting."

The transition Korman underwent in moving from Broadway to Madison Avenue was not only on a professional level but was mirrored in his personal life. Before opening the cafe society studio, Korman lived near his Mayfair Theater building in a hotel occupied by "Broadway characters, fight managers and stray tourists." Mornings found him making his way to nearby Lindy's diner for breakfast."[60] But once he opened the new studio, his world changed and he rented a small, quiet apartment above the Madison Avenue studio. And as Broadway gave way to Madison Avenue, so Lindy's gave way to Armando's, an upscale restaurant on 55th Street near Park Avenue, "jammed with chattering girls of the non-working class. Murray greets many of them in his best Park Avenue manner. He contributes to their pet charities and does a lot of free photographic work for their society benefits."[61]

And so, for almost two decades, Korman simultaneously ran two of New York City's most popular studios. Korman's career had turned another corner and likewise, his lifestyle turned a corner.

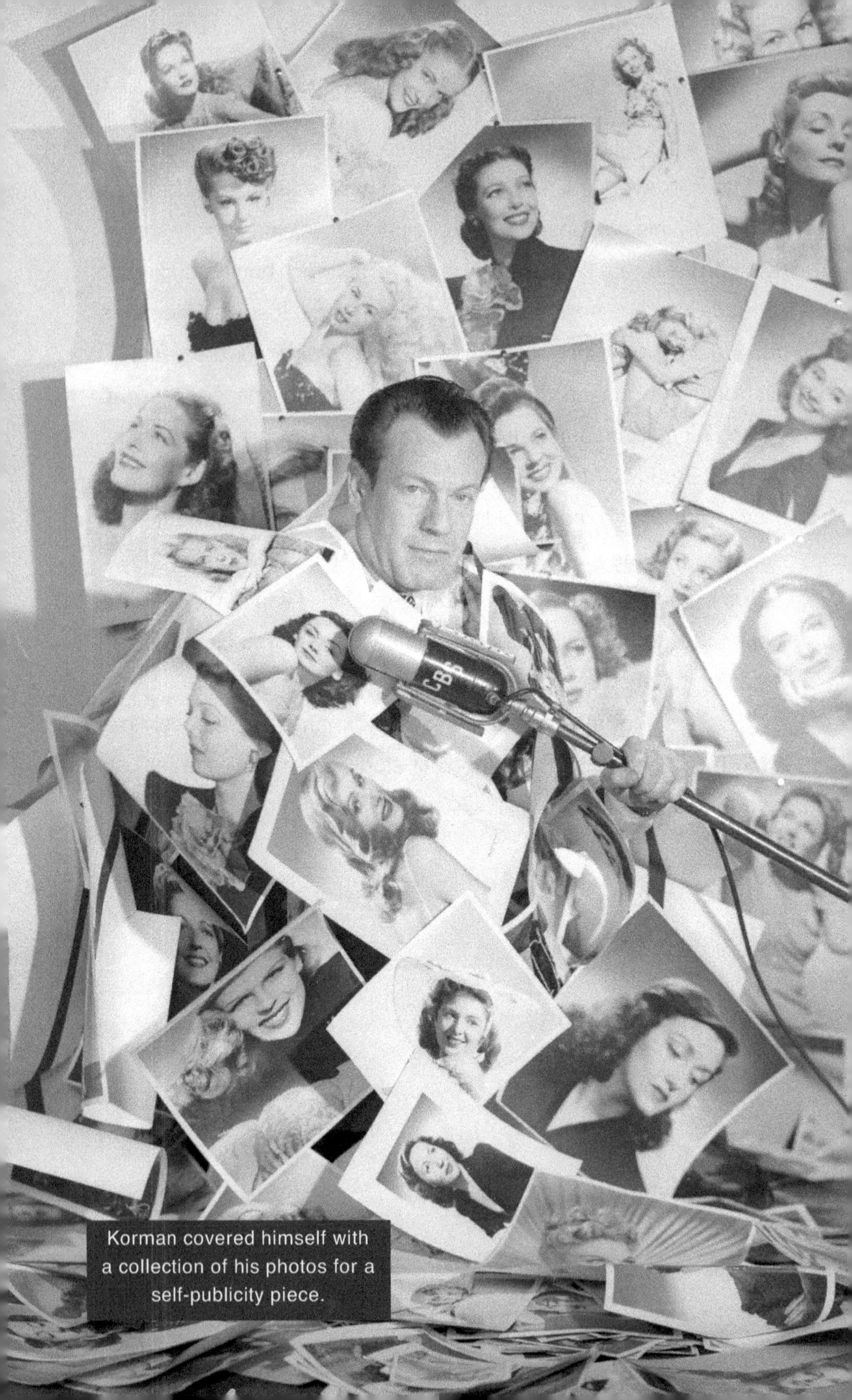

Korman covered himself with a collection of his photos for a self-publicity piece.

– CHAPTER 4 –

SUCCESSES AND SETBACKS

Though by all measures Korman's second location was a success, his enduring fame is more directly associated with his Broadway studio and its clients. These, primarily from the theatrical district – actors, actresses, and entertainers – found their way to Korman Studios by a variety of means. Many would-be entertainers came on their own dime, hoping Murray's artistry would provide the perfect, effective, public relations piece for distribution to prospective model and ad agencies. "He glamorizes those who want to be glamorized because they feel that these pictures help to get a job as a night club singer, model or actress" reported the *Arizona Republic* in a June 1941 article.

But others who found themselves waiting their turn in front of Korman's camera at his Broadway location were already stars or rising stars sent by their studio. These studios included the likes of Warner Brothers, Paramount, and United Artists, who often sent the entire cast from their Broadway plays.[62] It was by this avenue that Korman became the "official picture-taker for Ziegfeld."[63] So successful was he at glamorizing these stars of New York City's entertainment establishments that it was once rumored Hollywood, "ever on the alert for one who can enhance the attractions of their stars and starlets, is likely to offer him an opportunity to try his methods on [their] greats."[64]

One source noted that "[Korman] numbers every cabaret in town among his clientele."[65] This stream of starlets through his doors prompted one journalist to write that "perhaps in the entire country there is not another male who is on speaking terms with so many beautiful women."[66]

But Korman's subjects were not limited to those sent to him or those who sought him out. Some he sought out himself. It was not uncommon for Murray, while in a cab on his way to Lindy's for breakfast, to suddenly shout "Follow that girl!" Once the cab caught up with the unsuspecting beauty, Korman would step out, remove his hat "with a courtly gesture," then promptly hand her a business card bearing the address of Korman Studios. On the back of the card, he'd scribble "Come see me–M.K.." With equal expedience, Murray would hop back in the cab, drive away, leaving the startled young lady to wonder what just happened.

———●———

Korman made it his practice to retain copyright to every photo he shot. He would then sell duplicates to newspapers across the country who paid five to ten dollars for a small photo and several hundred for larger images used for their front pages. This is the avenue that arguably was responsible for having the greatest impact on Korman's rise to fame. For three decades, rare was the American newspaper that did not, at some point, publish one of his photos, always with credit given to "Murray Korman" and also branded with his trademark signature.

But his fame was not limited to America. Prior to WWII, Korman's images appeared in many foreign publications. One lucrative overseas contract he negotiated was with the The House of Carreras, a tobacco business in London, England. To "encourage repeat purchases and establish brand loyalty," tobacco companies inserted cards, featuring photos of popular cricketers, footballers, and film stars, into its cigarette packets.[67] These 68 x 36mm collector's items, with massive print-runs that often ran into hundreds of millions for each series,[68] are still sought after by avid collectors. Korman's beauties graced a Carreras series in 1939.

And then there was the request made by the German periodical, *Das Kleines Magazin*. Shortly before the United States entered the war, representatives from the magazine contacted Korman asking for pictures of "outstanding Broadway beautiful girls." Though still early in the conflict that would explode into WWII, rumors of Hitler's persecution of Jews had reached the states. Korman accepted the assignment with ulterior motives. He gathered what he considered the fifteen most beautiful Jewish chorus girls in New York, "photographed them from all angles," and promptly sent the photos overseas. *Das Kleines* returned them, "as Korman had fully expected, with a rather curt note to the effect that they were artistic but unacceptable."[69]

And so it was that in time, editors across the country came to accept Korman as an authority on beauty. According to a *New York Times* article, "through the years [Korman] was often called upon by the more sprightly publications[a] to choose 'the ten most beautiful girls in America' and prepare layouts of their pictures for publication."[70] His association with beautiful women was so pervasive that, in May 1935, Korman was called to testify before the New York Supreme Court as an expert witness in the field of feminine beauty. The case involved a popular Broadway showgirl, Eileen Wenzel, who was disfigured in an automobile accident. When the judge asked Korman "... as a photographer of beauty, to define that quality described as beauty"[71] he responded, "Well, it's perfect features, plus complexion and charm, ... and an expression — an expression you can't acquire. You are born with it, but may lose it." Eileen sued for $250,000 but, despite Korman's testimony, the case was declared a mistrial.[72]

But with success in any endeavor, there's a growing probability of an equal or greater amount of adversity. It can come in the form of well-meaning family and friends, jealous competitors, shrewd charlatans, or any other of a myriad of sources. Korman was no exception.

In the Spring of 1930 the wealthy socialite Barclay H. "Buzzy" Warburton (the same Warburton mentioned on page 30), rebounding from a failed marriage as well as other personal and

a The *Popular Photography* article (November 1937) used for a primary source for this story refers to a "newspaper syndicate" as the requester of Korman's "ten beauties of the year."

professional failures, exclaimed to reporters his intentions to become a photographer for the Social Register. Armed with a common, box Kodak camera, Buzzy shared that, "I intend to make my own living by taking photographs of socially prominent persons–my friends–and selling them to magazines." He went on to tell the gathered reporters that he had formed a partnership with Murray Korman.

When questioned about this partnership, Korman indicated that it had been considered, but would not be in his best interest. Besides, the young Buzzy owed Korman $2,500 for a pastel portrait, and he was having trouble collecting.[a] It's uncertain if Murray ever collected the money, but it's certain no partnership was formed.[73]

And then there was the Broadway dancer turned embalmer who, in 1935, sued Korman for $25,000. Full-page articles appeared in papers across the U.S. telling of how, to make a better living for herself, Frances Mildern took courses in embalming. She eventually gained her license and was practicing when photos that Korman took years prior, when she danced the stages of Broadway scantily clad, appeared in a "motion picture 'fan' magazine" without her permission. She argued that this damaged her professional reputation as an embalmer. The court eventually ruled in Korman's favor. It's very likely that the publicity Korman gained greatly offset his attorney's fees.

In the field of creative arts, where subjectivity rules, all artists encounter critics and Korman was no exception. Some criticized

a This is the same individual mentioned on page 28.

his style, characterizing him in disparaging tones as the original publicity "cheesecake" photographer. And there were those who believed his quantity compromised his quality, saying his studio was "more mass than class." And though many spoke of his likable personality, there's little doubt that the charismatic Korman could have rubbed some the wrong way. He was his own man. This and his phenomenal success surely spawned detractors and created ongoing rivalries between fellow photographers. Probably the most contentious rivalry was with a photographer named Bruno Bernard, better known as Bruno of Hollywood. One particular encounter with Bruno made the paper in October 1942. The brief blurb in The *Daily News* speaks of a "screaming match" between Bruno and Murray.

Ten years his junior, Bruno, like Korman, was a first-generation immigrant of Jewish descent, born into poverty. But Bruno's path to America began in Germany, during the reign of Adolph Hitler. In 1937, he fled to America from Nazi Germany, claiming to German authorities that he was leaving the country to continue his graduate studies.[74] He settled in California where he briefly attended the University of California, Berkeley. With aspirations to become a movie director, he soon became a directorial apprentice at the Reinhardt School of the Theatre in Los Angeles.

When unable to land a job, Bruno eventually abandoned his dream of becoming a director and reverted to his interest in photography. One source says that Korman was responsible for teaching him the tricks of the trade.[75] If true, this could be a major factor for the rivalry and explain why Bruno specialized in glamour photography. But, as his name implies, Bruno was based in Hollywood, though he made his way to New York on occasion. This is made certain by the publicized shouting match, but also by an event that took place about a month later, following the death of another photographer, Bill Stein. Stein's passing prompted the two, Korman and Bruno, to set aside their differences for a greater cause. "Everybody liked him...liked him so greatly that when he died, his chief business rivals, Murray Korman and Bruno toured Broadway collecting dough...They raised $652 which will pay for his funeral, a few small debts and will leave a little over for his family."[76] It would be easy to speculate that the heated rivalries, particularly from Korman's perspective, was more for public consumption (public relations) and less a true, bitter rivalry.

A second, and potentially the most contentious relationship was with the successful James J. Kriegsmann, owner of Kriegsmann Studio. In one publication he was referred to as Murray's "bitterest enemy."[77] This was certainly great fodder for the gossip columnist, but by all accounts Kriegsmann and Korman had not only a mutual respect for each other, but developed a close, personal friendship that would reap rewards for Murray in the latter years of his life.

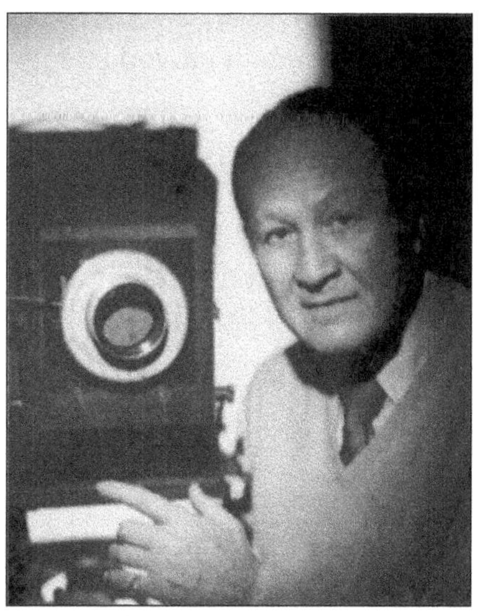

James Kriegsmann

Seven years his junior, James Kriegsmann immigrated from Vienna, Austria in 1929, and settled in New York City. Four years later he opened his photography studio on at 165 West 46th St., specializing in portraiture, eventually becoming the largest headshot photography studio in the world.[78]

The business grew to fill two floors of the Actors' Equity Building where Kriegsmann, unlike many contemporaries, put equal emphasis on his lab as his studio. According to his son, James Kriegsmann, Jr., what separated his father from many others in his profession, particularly Korman, was his business savvy. His father was a very good photographer, but Korman was as good, if not better, and admittedly "more artistic."[79] By contrast, though Korman had an entrepreneurial bent and a drive to succeed, in the end his business acumen proved suspect.

In 1988 Kriegsmann sold his business to a large lab. By this time his sons James Jr. and Tom had joined the business. The sales agreement with the purchaser allowed the brothers to retain a small studio space rent free. But soon both brothers struck out on their own.

In the Broadway world of glitz and glamour, where fortunes were often made at the expense of the naive and innocent, it would be easy to question the motives of any and every person involved in the entertainment industry. Few questioned Korman's artistic talent, but there's a great probability that many of Korman's critics questioned his motives. In that regard, a *Popular Photography* article from 1937 sheds an interesting light on Korman:

The fact that so many of "his girls" have made good is a source of sincere satisfaction to this cameraman who likes to think that his photographs have helped them gain recognition. In this he is quite justified – for photographs play an important part in getting a girl a chance in the movies, and where the ability to photograph well is obviously essential. The advertising agency, another great consumer of girlish charm, must see unusual pictures before it will give a model a chance.

Another way in which the photographer greatly assists the would-be glamour girl is by slanting publicity pictures so that they will appeal to the newspaper and magazine editors. For this, Korman has an uncanny and infallible ability. In a way, he feels a great responsibility toward his subjects. Almost every day some youngster, trying hard to break into a stage or screen career, comes to him with her meager savings which she has decided to spend on the set of photographs she hopes will start her on the path to success. Then, as he always does, the photographer plays the lights and lens on her to the best of his ability. Ten-to-one, a generous impulse will best him and he'll charge but a fraction of his usual high fee. "There is a higher reward than a financial one in knowing that I have helped some talented kid get the start she deserves in this tough racket they call show business," he exclaims. "Ten times the cash I get

> couldn't give me the same kick." If he thinks the girl is a comer he will do everything he can to put her on the right track, and show-world impresarios can thank him for many "finds" he has sent their way.[80]

As well stated in a *PIC* magazine article: "Korman's signature on a lobby photo is an indication of recognition for a showgirl. On a debs' photo it establishes her as a beauty."[81]

In the final analysis, Korman's early career focus of pencil and pastel portraits, as well as the beauty evident in his work, proved his artistic worth. Christine Trotter argued in Murray's defense in her essay *Murray Korman with Salvador Dalí, Dream of Venus,*[82] "Korman has been characterized as a publicity photographer and his studio 'more mass than class.' Yet Korman put his study at the Cooper Union for the Advancement of Science and Art in New York City to good use by creating memorable and sometimes sensual photographs of many of the top entertainers of the mid-twentieth century...Korman's popular appeal and distinctive lighting were joined with Salvador Dalí's imaginative, esoteric, and startling expressions to create an intriguing set of images for [The World's Fair exhibit,] the *Dream of Venus.*"[83]

The reasons behind Korman's eventual selection of genre and medium were noble. Korman thought beauty was as elevated an art form as painting. He believed "Art is an endeavor through composition to charm the senses. Real feminine beauty, proudly displayed, graciously displayed, achieves this."[84] His argument was seconded when in 1939 his work was included in the New York Library's Theatre Collection.[85]

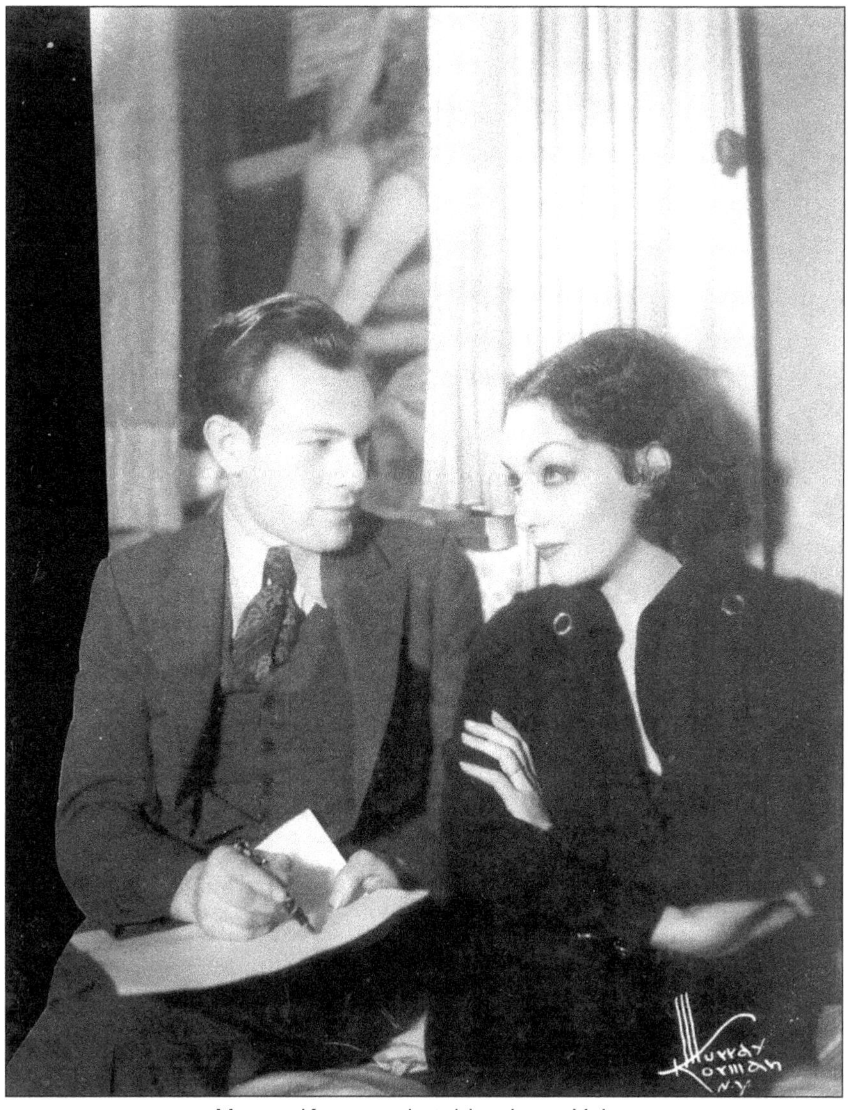

Murray Korman sketching Lupe Velez

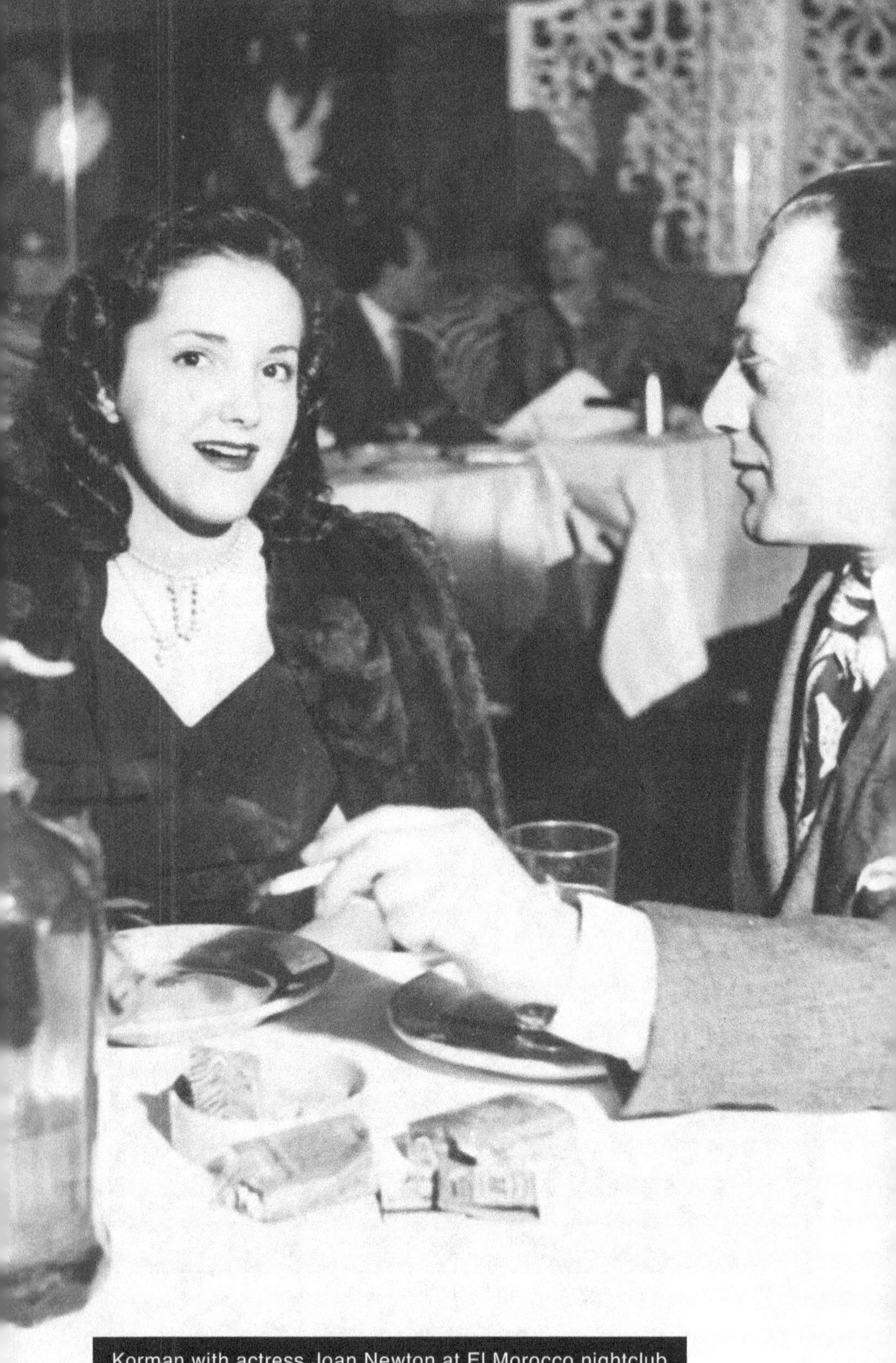

Korman with actress Joan Newton at El Morocco nightclub

– CHAPTER 5 –

MAKING A NAME

Korman's creative talent was without a doubt the primary impetus behind all he achieved. How else can one explain his early successes? But an in-depth look and analysis of his life reveal that turning his talent into a lucrative business could be attributed to more than sheer artistic abilities. Murray's entrepreneurial skills included a knack for promoting himself and his craft. This was achieved through various means. One avenue to this end was to simply find a way to rub elbows with New York's movers and shakers, and Korman accomplished this in a big way. He enjoyed an active social life and surely understood that a price tag could not be put on the publicity gained by running in the appropriate social circles. At the height of his career it was a rare week that his name did not appear in numerous gossip columns across the country, alongside many of the rich and famous of the era.

Most columnists of the era simply wrote about Korman, but one of the most popular developed a close friendship with Murray. Lee

Mortimer became both friend and confidant to Korman. Like Korman, Lee was the son of an Eastern European (Ukraine) immigrant, Nathan Lieberman. Nathan came to America in 1873, met and married Swedish immigrant Rose, and settled in Chicago. In 1904 they gave birth to their first child, Mortimer Lieberman who eventually adopted the pen name, Lee Mortimer.

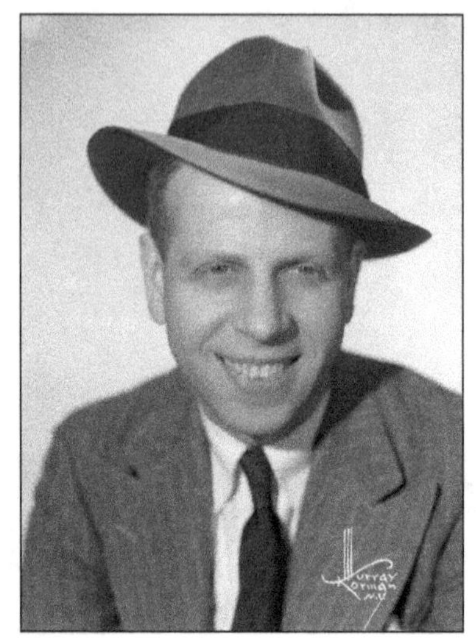
Lee Mortimer

Around 1930, after attending Northwestern University in Evanston, Illinois, Lee Mortimer moved to New York City where he found employment as an editor for *Amusements Magazine*. In 1932, he began a long-term association with the *New York Mirror*, working for editor Jack Lait.[86] His initial assignments at the *Mirror* were as a reporter and critic, eventually taking up his pen to be a Broadway gossip columnist. There's no documentation to verify it, but his role as gossip columnist very likely is what initiated the association and friendship with Korman.

Though best known as a columnist, over time Mortimer wore many different hats around New York City. Relationships that were developed over time opened doors for him to host his own jazz radio program. He also co-authored, with Lait, several bestselling crime books. Following that success, Mortimer began lecturing on crime and communism, and at one point attempted to tie popular singer Frank Sinatra to the Mafia and the Communist Party. This led to a face-to-face confrontation in Hollywood that made headlines.[87]

But it might be his work as associate editor for a short lived magazine, *Real Screen Fun,* that most closely tied him with Korman on a professional basis. Tilsam Publications' *Real Screen Fun* first appeared in 1935. When the debut issue rolled off the presses the interior was filled with sepia-tone photos of celebrities as well as all the latest gossip in the world of entertainment. It sold for 20 cents a copy and featured Korman's work heavily throughout its 64-pages. Furthering his exposure, the January 1936 issue contained a captioned picture of Korman posing with a group of people who were associated with motion pictures.

Though heavily featured in this publication, Korman appears to have no ties other than being one of several photographers whose works were included. But this exposure, among others, whetted an appetite referenced earlier: Korman wanted to get into publishing. And though his career path never carried him full-fledged into the field, his talent with the camera opened doors for dabbling in that world, and it proved an ideal tool for the promotion of himself and his photography. It's unclear what his official involvement was with most of these publications, but Korman's name was eventually attached to many of them, all pertaining to the entertainment industry and all showcasing his photography.

One of the earliest was the 50-page *Sheer Folly Magazine*, first published in 1937. Proudly displayed on the cover was the sub-headline "Photographs by Murray Korman, The World's Best Known Photographer of Beautiful Women." Far less polished but more risqué than *Real Screen Fun,* printed on cheap newsprint quality paper and smaller in size, *Sheer Folly Magazine* sold on newsstands for 15 cents a copy.

SNAP: Shots of Life with Laughs magazine, 10 cents per issue and tabloid size, hit the newsstands in August 1940. Korman shared space in this magazine with other photographers. Snap Publishing Company was based in Mt. Morris, Illinois but had editorial offices in NYC. *SNAP* had the same flavor as todays *People Magazine*.

Just two months later, debuting in October 1940, came the tabloid-size *"IT" That Personality Magazine*. Ten cents an issue, or the subscription price of $1.20 per year, with content very much like *SNAP*, this magazine was heavily populated with Korman photography. The back cover featured a full-page ad for Murray Korman Studios that beckoned New York City visitors to "avail

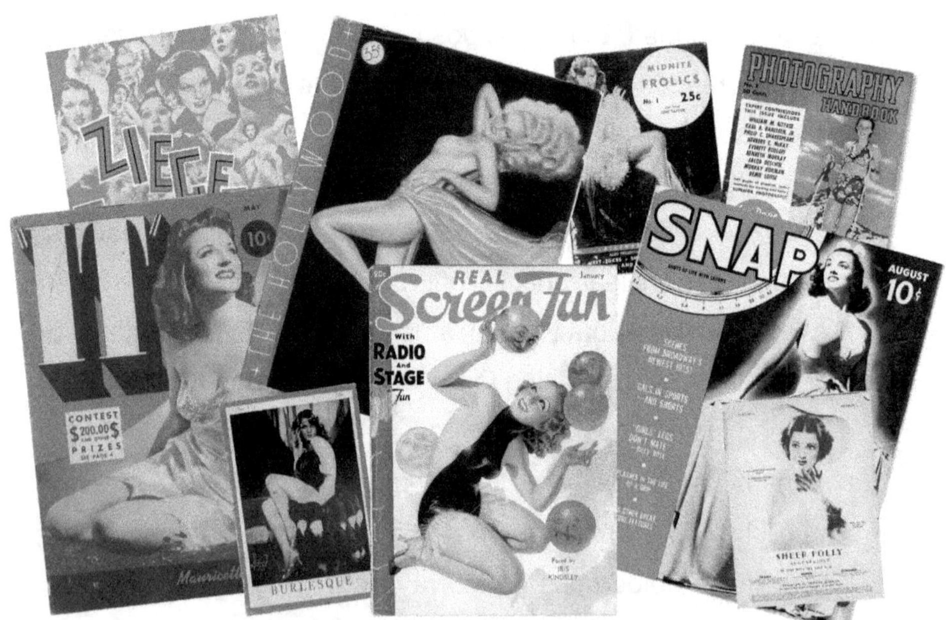

Some of the many publications that featured
Murray Korman and his photography

yourself of this opportunity to visit the Murray Korman Studios to get acquainted and be photographed in the modern manner." Page eighteen of the second issue, November 1940, featured a two-page article and photo of Korman himself.

And then there was the low-budget *Midnite Frolics* magazine. Relatively small at 7 x 9.5 inches, black and white throughout, this 26-page publication was by far the most risqué and clearly had soldiers as its target audience. The first issue, indicated by the simple "No. 1" on the cover, filled with military themed jokes and anecdotes, selling for 25 cents per copy, featured Murray Korman photos exclusively. One of the prominent features was a center-fold, much like girly magazines of today but far less revealing, that surely found their way into foot lockers and duffel bags of soldiers from the Atlantic to the Pacific. Interestingly, the entire publication is void of any mention of the publisher, issue numbers, issue dates, or any other information pertinent to it's creators.

Similar in many ways was *Burlesque*, though it was not targeted toward GIs. It was a small magazine which contained no photos on the inside pages, just humorous stories and comics, but it did have Korman's work on the front and back cover. Slightly smaller than *Midnite Frolics,* it also made no reference to its creator.

But Korman's most successful foray into the world of publishing appears to have been several years earlier than *Real Screen Fun*, and came by way of the Hollywood Restaurant, mentioned earlier. More nightclub than restaurant, it was birthed during the days of prohibition– at least on paper. It was then that

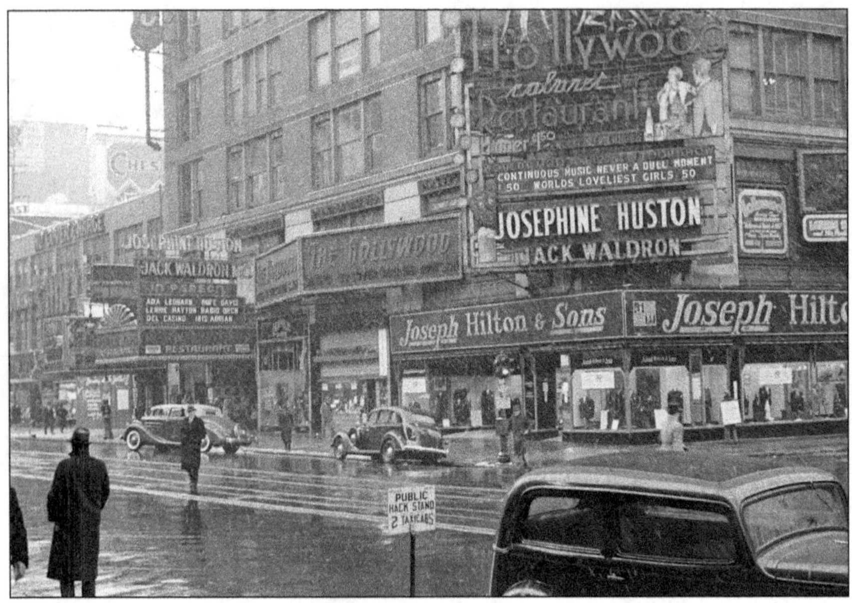

The Hollywood Restaurant

Joe Moss, a "nightclub man," considered the idea of combining a nightclub experience with a dining experience. Joining forces with Jacob Amron, a successful restaurateur, they found a suitable location that would accommodate one thousand diners, decorated it luxuriously, hired a full orchestra, signed some the most popular talent of the day, and set dinner prices at an affordable $1.50 and $2.00. Opening night in 1929 found the venue filled to capacity, with thousands being turned away. Joe Moss' plan was an immediate success, and Korman benefited significantly.

Early in its formation, Murray was contracted as the official photographer and sketch artist of the restaurant. And it's uncertain when, but they eventually offered their patrons a first-class souvenir program, titled appropriately *The Hollywood.*[a]

a The earliest issue the author located was dated 1934.

By far the most polished publication to showcase the work of Korman, *The Hollywood* could not be purchased at the corner newsstand, but was sold on location. The large program, printed on glossy paper, featured both photos and sketches of the restaurant's current entertainers, and every image was the work of Murray Korman. And it appears as if Korman may have been responsible not only for supplying the photos and sketches, but oversaw the program's production and printing. A blurb printed on the inside of the front cover reads "For additional copies write Murray Korman Studio's, 710 - 7th Ave. New York City."

Korman also recognized and took advantage of other opportunities to promote himself. One intriguing, though less notable, opportunity came when the New Jersey Raritan Photographical Society asked Korman to be a guest lecturer. *The Central New Jersey Home News* article's headline of February 3, 1937, read "Murray Korman Speaks to Club - Noted New York Photographer To Give First Lecture Here."

And there was the time that the Photographic Society, formed at a Naval Hospital at St. Albans, New York, offered Korman the opportunity to give lessons to wounded servicemen. It was in February 1948 that Murray, accompanied by one of his beautiful clients, gave free lessons to wounded servicemen in the hospital. Korman's personality was such that there's no doubting his sincerity in this act of kindness, nonetheless, it provided priceless publicity. [a]

---

a At the time of publication, a rare video of this encounter can be viewed at https://www.britishpathe.com/video/hospital-photographic-society.

Yet it could be argued that the most ingenious, yet subtle way Korman's reputation spread was simply by a stroke of luck. As mentioned earlier, editors from across the country began to consider Murray as an authority when it came to beauty. So, as one publication put it, he became a "self-described beauty expert" and took full advantage of the title. This paved the way for years worth of free publicity. The earliest recorded opportunity of him taking advantage of this was in the November 11, 1934 issue of the *Minneapolis Star Tribune*. Their 2-page, eye-catching article splashed the bold headlines "A Broadway Experts 4 'Perfect Beauties'–and Why." The article's author wrote, "Into the perpetual controversy as to who are the most beautiful women in the world steps Murray Korman, Broadway photographer, with standards that are distinctly those of New York, plus a background of close-up study of most of the lovely young women before the public today." For many years after, newspapers from across the country published full-page, or multi-page articles touting the country's most beautiful ladies selected by Korman, and accompanied by a liberal number of Korman's photos. Taking full advantage of this opportunity, whether intentional or not, the "beauties" were from all over the U.S. Thus, when a hometown girl made the list, local newspapers from El Paso to Akron to Omaha ran articles on their hometown beauty, accompanied by Korman's photography.

To further capitalize on his title of beauty expert and all his success in the world of glamour photography, Korman offered to share his knowledge of the trade to anyone willing to pay. In 1947 he self-published a series of five pamphlets entitled, *The Art of*

Glamour Photography. Sold as a "course," it cost $10 and presented his analysis of poses, lighting, and difficulties photographing certain parts of the anatomy.[88] He was also called upon to share tricks of the trade and write how-to articles published in numerous magazines such as *Photography Handbook* and *Popular Photography.*

It was not long after the opening of his second studio that Korman landed possibly his most publicized and enduring project. The opening of the 1939 World's Fair, an economic and publicity boom for both New York City as well as Korman, featured the Dream of Venus pavilion designed by Salvador Dalí. Renowned photojournalist Eric Schaal was called on to photograph the actual exhibit, but George Platt-Lynes, Horst P. Horst, and Korman were hired to shoot publicity photos, under the art direction of Dalí. These photos, housed in Hofstra University Library Special Collections, remain some of Korman's most popular work.

Another major attraction and "hit of the fair" was Billy Rose's Aquacade, "a spectacular musical and water extravaganza foreshadowing the form of many popular Hollywood musicals in the ensuing years. The show was presented in a special amphitheater seating 10,000 people and included an orchestra to accompany the spectacular synchronized swimming performance."[89] Rose, a theatre and nightclub owner with whom he had previously worked on Broadway, hired Korman to provide all of the publicity photos of their swimmers. At this time, two of America's most celebrated athletes were swimmers Johnny Weissmuller and Eleanor Holm, both of whom participated in the Aquacade. To date, the photos of Holm and Weissmuller are some of the most sought after works of Korman's.

Interestingly, Korman and Dalí had made headlines two years prior to the World's Fair, due to a more contentious encounter. To say Korman was an outspoken critic of Dalí's surrealist style is an understatement. It was on January 9, 1937, that Murray encountered Dalí at a New York art gallery, intending to voice his opinion. The exact circumstances are unknown, but he later confessed they were orchestrated. When the opportunity presented itself, he made the best of it and for fifteen minutes he and Dalí bantered back and forth. The only problem was that Dalí did not understand English and Murray didn't understand French. Eventually, Dalí asked an interpreter to intercede, and the exchange went like this:

"It's a big fake," said Korman

"What's a big fake?" asked the interpreter.

"This surrealist show," said Korman.

The interpreter passed this on to Dalí, who raised an eyebrow.

"It's not art," Korman shouted at the eyebrow.

The interpreter intercepted.

"Mais, oui!" said Dalí.

The interpreter explained this meant, "Sure, I know it."

"It's morbid," said Korman. "It's a bad influence. It will spread."

The interpreter stepped in again and relayed Dalí's reply:

"Bon."

The interpreter said this meant, "Swell. I'm glad to hear it."

To quote an article that recorded details of the exchange,

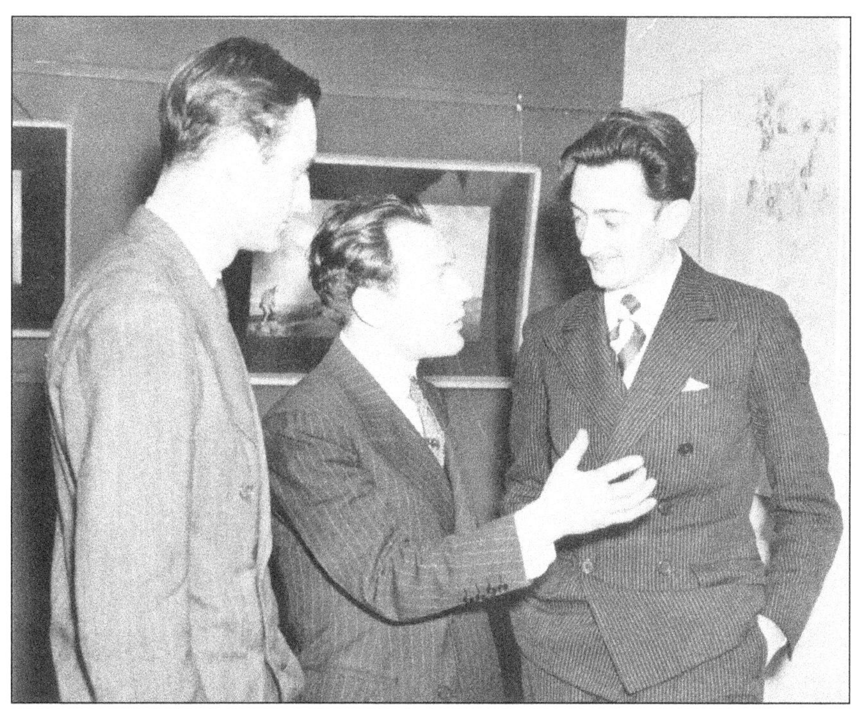

Korman (middle) confronts Dalí (right),
with interpreter Julien Levy (left)

"Korman left in disgust, for he confided to reporters he had planned to 'show this guy up.'"[90] An Associated Press article that appeared in *The Tennessean Sun* on January 17, reporting on the encounter, summed it up with the headline "Surrealist Dismays Critic by Agreeing It Is Bad Influence." It would appear that though he "left in disgust," Korman got his message across despite the language barrier. And he may well have earned a certain amount of respect in light of the fact that several years later Dalí called on Korman to assist with the World's Fair project.

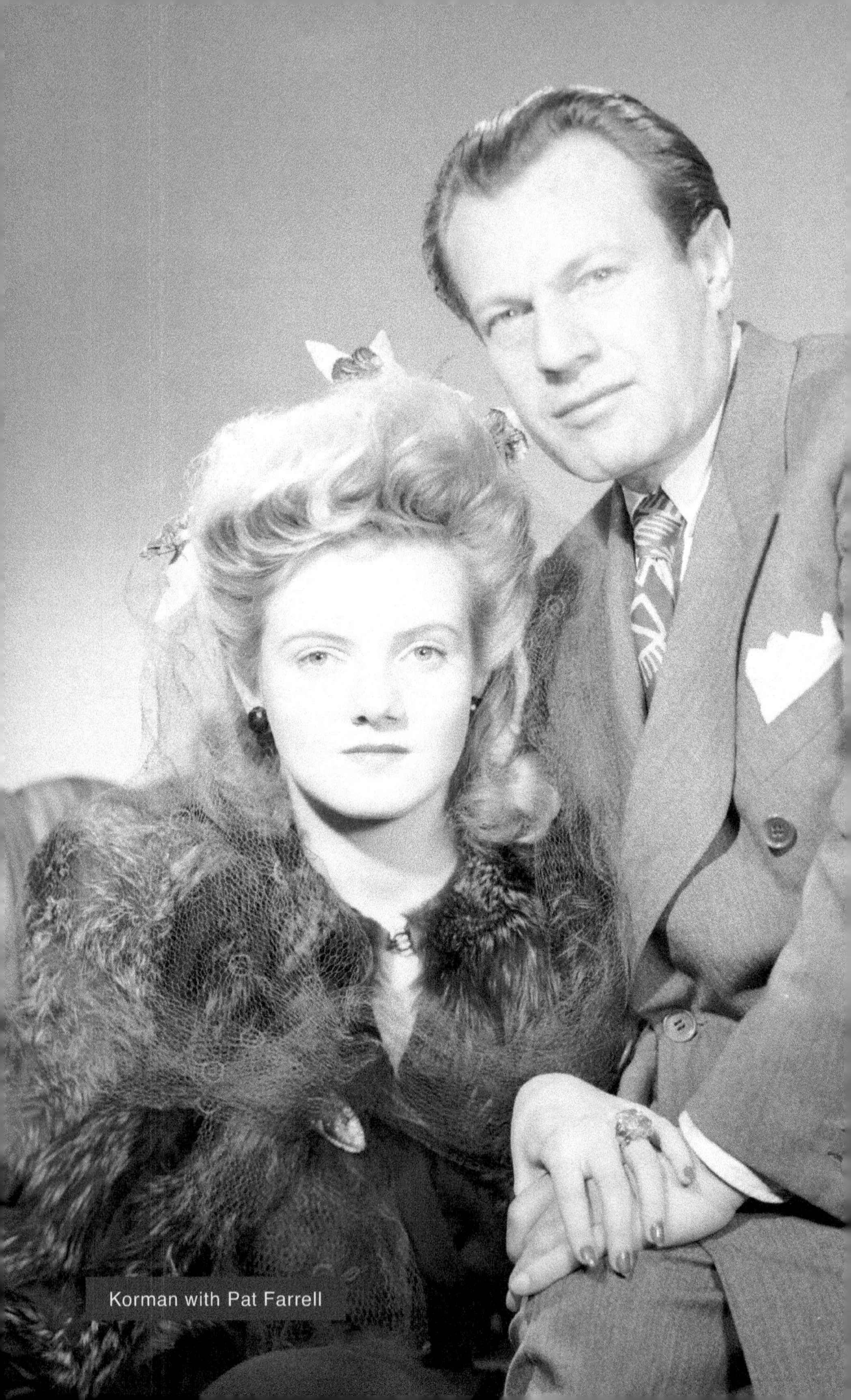

Korman with Pat Farrell

– CHAPTER 6 –

BIG NAME, BIG PERSONALITY

As discussed in the previous chapter, with fame came popularity, and Korman's social life rapidly followed the path of his professional successes. A testament to his having arrived socially was the frequency in which his name appeared in newspapers across the country, particularly in gossip columns. And Korman quickly found himself on the same social level as the era's most popular stars. Rumors abounded. The subjects of the rumors were varied but supposed relationships dominated most of the gossip. It was reported: "Another romance is that of Murray Korman and bricktopped Eleanor DeVan," "Murray Korman, the photog, and Ruth Miller are taking close-ups," Murray Korman...and Betty Bruse are posing for love scenes–and it isn't just a pose," "Murray Korman... wooing Virginia Stevenson," "Murray Korman and Dottie Dare a twosome," "Murray Korman, the Broadway beaut photographer...is saying 'Smile, please' to Ann Kerr," and "Murray Korman and Kiddy Kelly, the adorable comedienne, are playing artist and model."

The popular journalist Dorothy Kilgallen commented "One of my favorite Broadway characters is Murray Korman, the diminutive Lothario of the lens. He spends his days photographing beautiful chorines and torch singers and showgirls attired in wisps of tulle, strings of beads, or a picture hat–and he spends his evenings surrounded by the same kind of beauty, only more warmly wrapped. Never saw him without a pretty girl on his wing – and sometimes there are two or three."[91]

And Korman's lifestyle gave columnists plenty of material. *The New Yorker* reported that "Korman's life after working hours is spent almost entirely in night clubs. The ones he likes best are the Monte Carlo Beach and El Morocco. The Master's behavior in a nightclub is sometimes regarded as eccentric. ... Korman generally dominates the conversation of any group he is in. His chief subject is himself. He has never married, but he is frequently seen in the company of one or another of the girls he photographs, and he almost as frequently declares that he is engaged. To break the monotony of his nightclub regimen, he occasionally goes on beagling excursions and other outings with his society friends. They admire his democratic ways, his genius, and his ability to view himself with detachment." It was said of Korman that he became a "suave, voluble, and worldly figure around Lindy's."[92]

Korman's niece, Roberta Satro, recalled that "Murray would show up at [our] apartment with a showgirl on each arm, someone from the cafe society, or a millionaire. Women from all walks of life wanted to marry him — Broadway and cafe society alike."[93] And marriage was often the topic of Murray Korman gossip column blurbs. In a short but to-the-point blurb in July 1951, Kilgallen reported: "Murray Korman, the glamor photog, is on the verge of another waltz up the aisle – this time with Marilyn Monroe."[a] Years earlier, when asked about marriage, Korman said "I've been caught proposing now and then. Sometimes I've been accepted, but then the girl of the moment would start reflecting on all the sirens who are part of my daily routine. That always scares them off so I guess I'll end up becoming a monk."[94]

But Korman would eventually tie the knot. In the summer of 1943 rumors circulated with news of Murray's inevitable proposal to socialite Ann Kerr. But Ed Sullivan, in his column dated October 9 of that year, reported that "Korman showed me a ring which he says is for Pat Farrell's third digit." And so it was, on November 9, 1943,[b] Murray married Pat Farrell, a showgirl twenty-two years his junior,[95] sent to his studio from a local modeling agency.[96] It was not until a decade later that details surrounding the blessed event became public. An article by friend and columnist Lee Mortimer, dated December 29, 1953, records his first-person account of that evening:

> "For more than 20 years Murray Korman had been taking pictures of glamorous stage beauts and social debbies in various stages of dress and undress and mostly "un," but none lured him to the alter. It remained for Patricia Farrell, a fragile blonde from Brooklyn, who

---

a The author has found no evidence of a connection between Korman and the famous actress.

b There's a degree of uncertainty regarding the exact date of Murray and Pat's wedding. A photo taken at their reception appeared in the November 11, 1943 issue of *PM* newspaper and mentioned the wedding as having taken place "yesterday" which would give November 10 as the date. But Lee Mortimer gives a date of November 9.

had been sent to his studio by a models' agency, to snap the bracelets on his wrist and throw the key away. None of us on the Apple ever thought we'd live to see that day, because after photographing some 10,000 of the nation's loveliest in the intimate poses known to the trade as "cheese-cake" we figured Murray was thoroughly anesthetized to what a bountiful nature gives babes to snag a meal-ticket."

"George Lait,....and I were the witnesses at the strange midnight ceremony performed in the Ft. Lee, N.J., police station by Judge Aronsohn, with Carl Erbe,

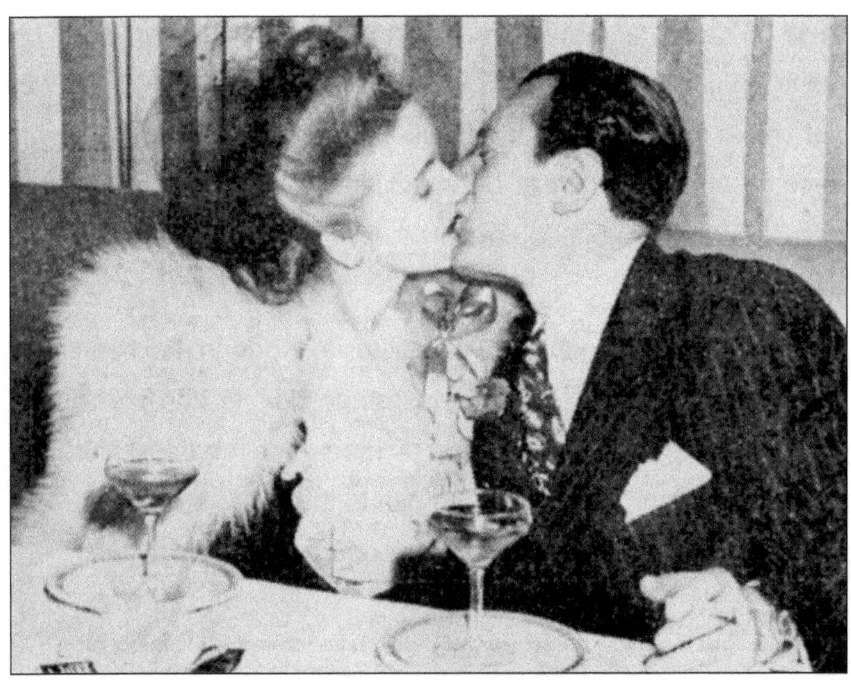

Korman and Farrell at their wedding reception, Cafe Zanzibar

> the noted publicist, acting as majordomo and master of ceremonies. The bride gave her age as 19 and produced a birth certificate to attest to the fact. The wedding date was Nov. 9, 1943, and it also was her birthday. Erbe was then interested in a cafe on Broadway known as the Zanzibar, and the marriage had been dreamed up in his fertile brain as a publicity stunt for the same. Though it was supposed to be secret, it was as secret as Adlai Stevenson's plans for '56 and Erbe invited the newspaper cameramen to the intimate wedding party at the Zanzibar."

Satro recalled a time when the couple was visiting their home and, at some point, Farrell slipped off to a bedroom and fell asleep. "Pat was beautiful; sleeping on the bed she looked like an angel," Roberta said.

It's worthy to note that, with all his fame and fortune, he never let success go to his head. He was very charismatic with a "fabulous personality" but never "impressed with himself."[97]

It's also worth noting that, according to a column in *The Honolulu Advertiser* dated January 29, 1944, by this time Korman had three studios. A Private John Young wrote the following inquiry to the newspaper's *Dear Miss Fixit*[a] column: "Is it possible that you could relay to me the address of Murrey[b] Kormans studios, located around Times Square section of New York City? It is famous for its photos of theatrical personalities." The columnist responded

a Miss Fixit was the pen name for *Honolulu Advertiser* columnist, Alicia Adams.

b Private Young misspelled Korman's first name.

"You betcha, John. Here 'tis: Murray Korman Studios (note correct spelling): They have three locations in New York City. They are: 675 Fifth Ave., 534 Madison Ave., and 701 Seventh Ave." And there would soon be a fourth location.

Whether or not it was a mere coincidence is up for debate, but after the marriage, Korman's life took several unfortunate turns. One of the most significant involved an apparent misunderstanding of Murray's intentions for life with his new bride. According to Mortimer, sometime during their courtship "seems Korman told his bride that 'I'll putcha in pitchures.' Of course, he meant in his studio pictures, but she thought he meant the movies and she held him to it."

And so it was that the newlyweds soon made their way to California where Pat, with Murray's support, embarked on the difficult task of building an acting career. Little is known about the timing or circumstances surrounding this move, but thanks to an ad in *The Los Angeles Times* it can safely be assumed that it took place within nine months after their wedding. On August 15, 1944, the following ad was published that read:

YES!
He is the Same
MURRAY
KORMAN
of Fifth Ave., New York.
"AMERICA'S FOREMOST
PHOTOGRAPHER"

> Where glamour in photography was originated. 500,000 ladies in every walk of life have been in front of his camera to date and now you are invited to be glamorized by him in his newly opened Studio at
> 7557 Sunset Blvd.
> HE. 5607
> Uncle Sam gave him a Super-Fortress–now you give him a Super-Portrait.

How all of this transpired remains a mystery but it's certain that Korman opened his fourth studio on the west coast mere months after the wedding. Lee Mortimer shared some insight behind the move: "A few months after his marriage Murray opened an ornate branch on Hollywood's not-so-glittering Sunset Strip where he planned to rake in the shekels taking portraits of film stars while Pat made a name for herself in the movies." But the greater mystery surrounds an ad, hidden in the for-sale classified ads of the same newspaper, printed September 1, 1944, less than a month after the original ad. It read as follows:

> PHOTOGRAPHIC STUDIO. Large. Fully equipped. Gd. loc. 7557 Sunset.
> HE-5607. Murray Korman.

Though the specifics behind the opening and sudden closing of the Hollywood location are unknown, they certainly coincide with

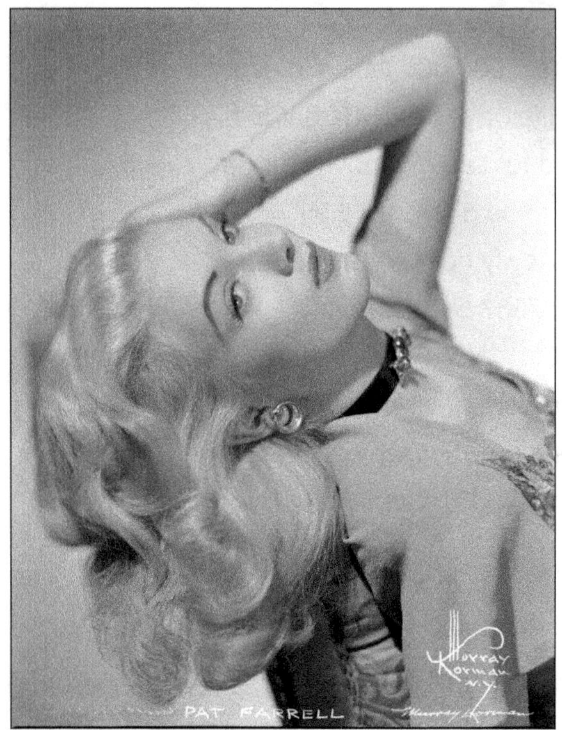

Pat Farrell

marriage troubles. Rumors of divorce began to circulate. Murray, though he said he still loved her, had returned to New York without Pat but continued supporting her by sending her $200 a week. Then, in Mortimer's words, "One night she phoned collect and said 'Murray, I love you. Wire me the fare. I'm coming back.'" A blurb in the *Daily News*, dated September 30, 1944, announced: "The Murray Kormans have kissed and made up." Upon Pat's arrival home Murray threw a combination welcome home and anniversary party at the El Morocco nightclub.

But the ups and downs of Korman's married life would continue for many years. In November, just weeks after returning home to Murray, Pat was signed by Dave Wolper for a part in a new Broadway musical, "Glad To See You."[98] The play flopped and closed, never opening in New York.[99] Almost as suddenly, in December 1944, the Kormans returned to Hollywood where it was reported that "film companies fell over each other giving Pat screen tests. But young Mrs. Korman wasn't interested."[100]

Though reported as uninterested in a career in Hollywood, by July Pat had returned once again, presumably by herself, and was "having a fling at the cinema."[101] She soon signed with Warner Brothers. And again, rumors of discontent were circulating, followed quickly by talk of divorce. At the center of this most recent storm of rumors was the heart-throb movie star, Errol Flynn.

Australian born Errol Flynn, after breaking into acting in Britain, appeared on the Hollywood scene in 1935 quickly landing prominent roles in several successful films. But his lead role in Warner Brother's *The Adventures of Robin Hood* (1938) catapulted him to global fame. By the time the Kormans began traveling to the west coast, Flynn's career was established and he was married to his second wife, Nora Eddington. But controversy and rumors persistently knocked at his door and by September rumors of a relationship with Pat Korman were flying from coast to coast. Considering both were currently working for Warner Brothers, and Flynn had already "developed a reputation for womanising,"[102] it's easy to assume their paths not only crossed but that there might be legitimacy to the rumors. Dorothy Kilgallen's *Voice of Broadway* column, dated September 20, 1945, read "Errol Flynn keeps his newest romance a secret from the Hollywood chatterers by having a friend call for her and take her home – but he sees her almost daily. She's blonde Pat Farrell, Broadway photog Murray Korman's estranged wife, now a picture starlet." Columnist Louis Sobol chimed in saying, "Society and Theatrical Photographer Murray Korman, a forlorn chap these days and nights...Says his pretty film-bride would never have left him if she hadn't become smitten with that certain dashing film actor...Korman says he's going to sue that certain d.f.a. for $500,000 for alienation, etc., etc.... Someone suggested that now that his heart is broken, his photography will probably reach the status of high art... 'Every time the camera clicks,' said Korman, mournfully, 'it's my heart beating for that girl.'"

Pat returned to New York on September 28 of that same year. Some thought it was to reconcile with Murray, others doubted. Gossip columns were alight with he-said, she-said. And so it went for almost 11 years, hitting its lowest point on September 19, 1950. Pat was admitted to New York City's Bellevue Hospital for an overdose of sleeping pills. Most columnists assumed it was intentional but Murray insisted the overdose was an accident, her having mistaken the pills for saccharine tablets. Ever the gentleman, and still in love, Murray stayed by her side through the ordeal only to see Pat leave him again in a matter of months.

Best described as a love-hate relationship, the marriage lasted until July of 1954 when the divorce became final.[103] The apparent straw that broke the camel's back was a much-publicized two-year affair Pat had with night club comedian Georgie Kaye. In December of 1953, Pat brought a paternity suit against Georgie claiming she was pregnant with his child.[a] In the meantime, Murray was in court as well, filing for absolute divorce, charging Pat with adultery.[104]

Mention of Pat slowly faded from the gossip columns. She remarried in July 1958 but never realized her dreams of fame and

a To date the author can find no records of Pat giving birth to a child.

fortune. And though rumors of matrimony circulated from time to time, Murray never walked down the aisle again. But for more than a decade the couple provided a career's worth of material for many New York gossip columnists.

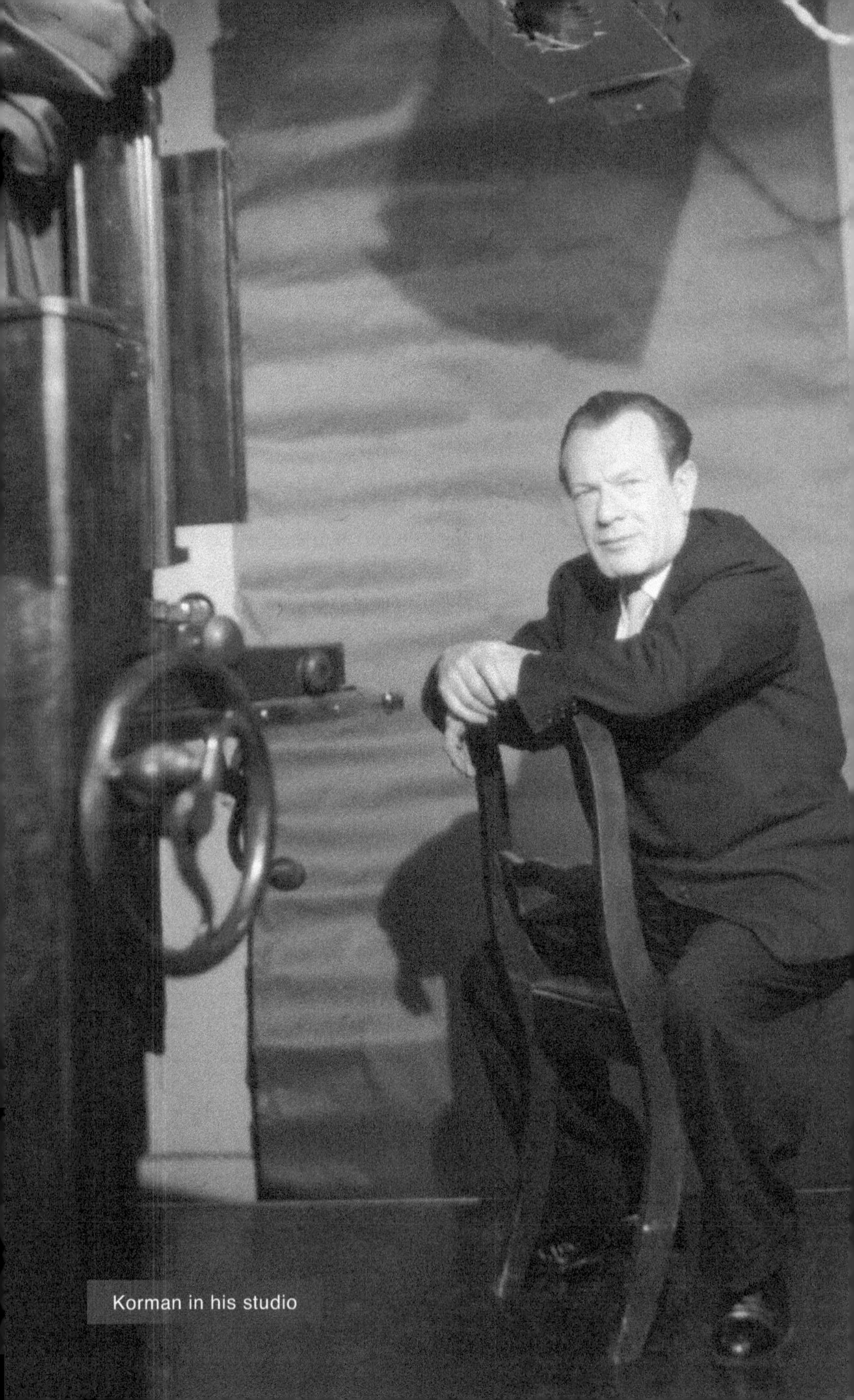
Korman in his studio

– CHAPTER 7 –

A QUIET END TO A LOUD LIFE

The factors that lead to Korman's professional and financial demise are as diverse as they are speculative, but there came a time in the life of Korman Studios when troubles compounded and the magic began to wane. Some sources point to employees who mismanaged his business affairs as the primary factor. Murray's overall cavalier approach to business, and his trusting of others to handle monetary concerns, not uncommon for one with an artistic bent, certainly did not serve him well. As discussed earlier, he was never punctual, keeping clients waiting for hours before showing up at the studio, a practice that most likely cost him business in the long run. And, it was not infrequent for a struggling, want-to-be actress to pull at his heartstrings and walk away paying little or nothing for Korman's expertise. And then there was his extravagant, spare-no-expense life style that eventually caught up with a dwindling bank account. Rare was the evening that he was not spotted at some nightclub or theater wining and dining any number of beautiful people. There were even quietly circulated rumors that accused employees, who were trusted with the company finances, of theft.

But the complex personal and financial issues associated with his troubled marriage were possibly the primary factor in Korman's difficult years. Pat influenced what appears to have been an impromptu move to California which surely had a negative impact on his New York studios. One can only imagine how the sudden opening and closing of the Hollywood location in 1944 took a toll on the company's bottom line. And though records can't be found to verify it, one source tells of Murray supporting Pat until her death, and then paying her funeral expenses.[a]

Compounding his financial and professional problems were family concerns. Both of his brothers died unexpectedly in the 1940s. Sol died December 27, 1941, and Harry passed away on December 15, 1948.

Korman navigated the troubled waters of the 1940s with relative success but the beginning of the next decade proved far more difficult. According to Korman's obituary[105] he "met reverses in 1950 and left New York to try his fortune in California." It's probably not incidental that this date coincides with a lawsuit that made headlines that same year. In May of 1950, a stripper by the name of Winnie Garrett sued Korman for $50,000 charging that he sold pictures of her to a penny-a-peep machine vendor causing her "mental anguish and distress."[106] (Two and a half years later the New York Supreme Court threw out the suit saying it had passed the statutes of limitations.) And it was in November of 1950 that Ed

a Several sources indicated that Pat committed suicide but no records were found to verify this.

Sullivan wrote in his column that "Murray Korman's file of negatives sold[a] at public auction."[107] The article gave no reason, but it's easy to assume they were sold to pay off debts.

Details regarding Korman's return to California are elusive, but soon he was back in New York. And compared to prior years, details surrounding this period of his life are scarce. But after two decades of remarkable success with his singular style of glamour photography, the post-war public was ready to head in a new direction. The entertainment industry as a whole was moving away from nostalgic and comical themes to the sleek post-war "international style," and so Korman's glossy images from another era were out of favor, and this reality compounded Korman's struggles.

Records are cloudy, but what is clear is that, relative to his earlier successes, the 1950s were unkind to Korman. And for the remainder of his career it appears that he relied heavily on other photographers for assistance.

How and when the partnership formed is unclear, but sometime during the 1950s Korman found himself "associated with the Gil Ross[b] photo studio at the Concord Hotel in the Catskills."[108] Murray and the very likable Ross, 18 years his junior, hit it off well, working together for much of the decade.[109] The studio was located at the hotel, but their darkroom was in a downstairs portion of his

a The source of Sullivan's claim is unknown. There might have been some truth to his comment, but after Korman's death in 1961 his heirs inherited a large number of negatives.

b According to an article published on vintagenewsdaily.com, "in the 1950s [Korman] formed a partnership with photographer Gil Ross and the joint studio operated at 32 West 58th Street in Manhattan." This information can't be verified and was contradicted by Mitch Ross, Gil's son, in a phone interview.

family's home in nearby Monticello. Korman's frequent trips to the Ross household, visiting the darkroom, helped create an enduring friendship.

The Catskills, consider by some to be America's "first great vacationland,"[110] had long been a destination spot for wealthier New York City residents looking to escape the city's summer heat. But it was the post-WWII 1940s and 1950s that saw the greatest boom in new resorts and tourism. And at the time Korman began working at the the 1,500-guest-room, 2000-acre Concord Hotel which was the largest resort in the area and considered a premier vacation spot in the entire Northeast. Known for its multiple, impressive entertainment venues it attracted major entertainers from across the country. Undoubtedly Ross and Korman, along with Ralph Oggiano, another renowned photographer/portraitist in the autumn of his career whom Ross had hired, provided concessionaire services unequaled in the Catskills. Herman Lewinter, a talented photographer in his own right, worked as their dark-room specialist.[111]

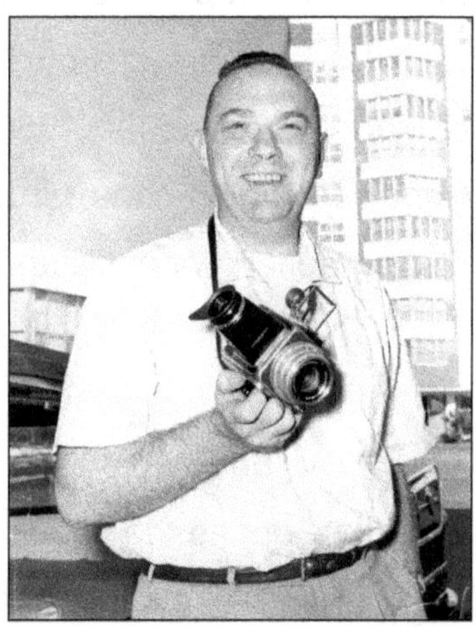
Gil Ross

It would have to be assumed that the 100-mile distance between New York City and the Concord's location in Kiamesha Lake, prevented Korman from simply commuting. He most likely found a temporary residence in Monticello because no records indicate a permanent move from New York City.

A Lee Mortimer article verifies that Korman worked at the Concord as late as July 1958: "Murray Korman...celebrated the remarriage of his ex-wife, Pat, with champagne at the Concord, where he's the photo studio concessionaire."[112] But by 1960 Korman was working as an independent photographer within the Kriegsmann studios.[a] Walter Winchell's column, *On Broadway*, dated August 1960, tells that Korman "moved back to the West Side – sharing a studio with his one-time bitterest enemy James Kriegsmann." Though there's little doubt that the two photographers competed for the same clientele, with equal certainty it can be said that there existed a great degree of professional, mutual respect between them. According to James Kriegsmann, Jr., "they were never, ever enemies. Everybody liked Murray. My father respected him and helped him when he needed help."[b] It was not uncommon for photographers to "form short-lived partnerships with other artists."[113] Regardless of the circumstances that brought him to this point, Korman, the man who was on top of the world in the 30s and 40s, struggled to find consistency and stability in his professional and personal life at this time.

But ever the entrepreneur, and with a contagious optimism, in 1960 Korman told columnist and friend Lee Mortimer that he had a

---

a In a phone interview with Mitch Ross, son of Gil Ross, he indicated Korman was still working with his father at the time of his death. This, as well as a documented 1955 hospital emergency room visit mentioned on the next page, leads the author to believe that the Catskills job was a part-time job. It's quite certain that Korman maintained a working relationship with Ross and the Concord Hotel, which accounts for the hotel's director of entertainment, Phil Greenwald, paying Murray's funeral expenses.

b During a phone interview with James Kriegsmann, Jr. in May, 2020, he vividly recalled meeting Murray and his wife, Pat Farrell. Since Pat and Murray had divorced in 1954, Murray and his wife would have been in the company of the Kriegsmann's family years before Murray worked in the Kriegsmann studio.

"firm deal to open a studio in London."[114] And in early August 1961, he confided in friends that "show people owed him $35,000 and if he could have collected, he'd have been in good shape financially."[115]

It was also during the difficult 1950s that Korman began to experience health issues. In April of 1955, he was rushed to Manhattan General Hospital, surviving a heart attack. Almost five years later, January 1960, found him in an upstate hospital suffering from pleurisy, presumably while working at the Concord. Then in January of 1961, Korman survived another heart attack.[116] James Kriegsmann, Jr., reflecting back on encounters with Murray during this time period noted that Korman looked very unhealthy. "Murray was definitely a chain smoker," recalled Kriegsmann.

It was a warm summer day, Wednesday, August 9, 1961, when Korman left his apartment at 44 W. 55th St. and, most likely following his decades-long routine of a late breakfast, chatting easily with friendly, familiar faces, made his way approximately nine blocks to the Kriegsmann Studio at 165 W. 46th St. It was here that Murray suffered a heart attack he would not recover from. He died on the job, doing what he loved most; capturing for time and posterity, the beauty of every person that had the privilege to sit in front of his lens.

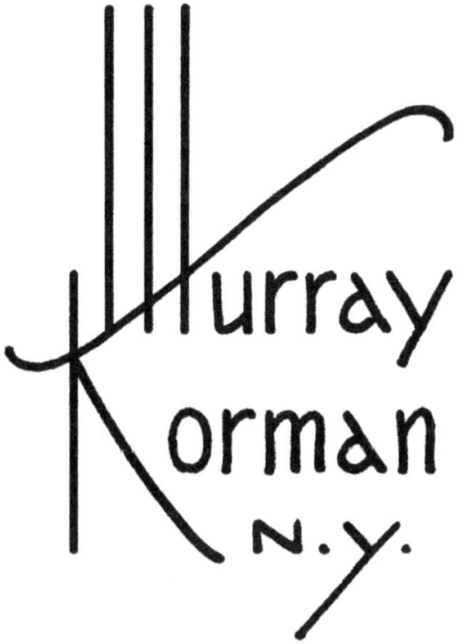
Murray
Korman
N.Y.

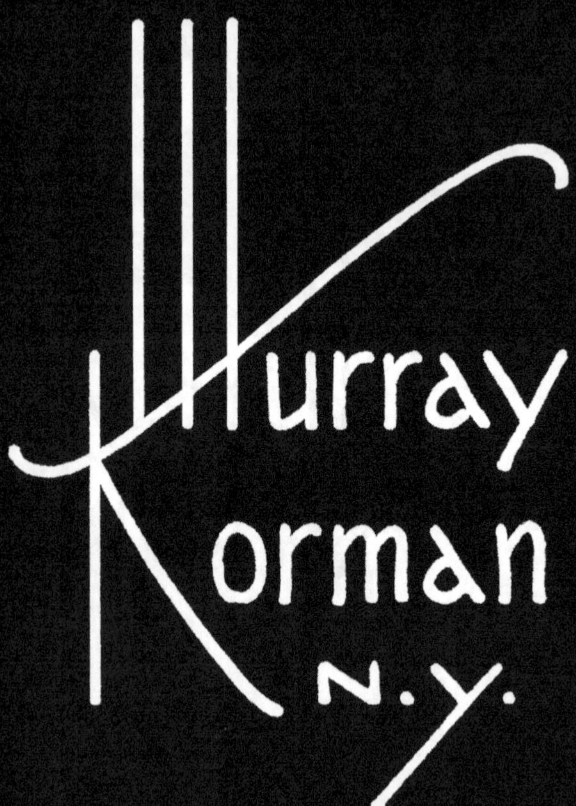
Murray
Korman
N.Y.

– CHAPTER 8 –

AFTERWORD

Korman's artistic gift and entrepreneurial skills earned him an enormous amount of respect, fame, and fortune, in spite of the disadvantages he inherited as a youth. Sadly he died penniless. During his last days, just to make ends meet, he was using borrowed camera equipment.[117] Phil Greenwald, director of entertainment at the Concord Hotel, paid Korman's funeral expenses.

Though not completely abandoned, at the time of his death Korman's friends and family were few and far between. Most of his immediate family predeceased him in death. As mentioned earlier, his two brothers, Sol and Harry, died in 1941 and 1948 respectively while his sisters, Jean and Dora, had passed away prior to 1959. The few relatives who were still alive had lost touch with him. An Associated Press article dated August 10, 1961 reported that "Helen Hall, Korman's friend for more than 30 years, said she knew of no relatives with whom he was in close touch." Despite their differences, Murray remained close to his ex-wife Pat Farrell after their divorce, but she had died an untimely death in her mid-thirties.[a] Korman's obituaries documented only two survivors: nieces Sally Greaves and Roberta Grill, both of the Bronx. Kriegsmann's employees and the few others close to Korman at the time of his death were unaware of any family, and failed to notify the nieces. It was not until after his funeral that they were informed that Murray had died.

Soon after, Kriegsmann had Korman's negatives delivered to his heirs. With no room to store them all, Grill and Greaves pored through the negatives, kept the ones they considered most valuable, boxed them up and stored them away. The rest were returned to Kriegsmann's studio.[118] It's uncertain what became of them after Kriegsmann sold his business in 1988.

And though the largest percentage of Korman's work is lost to time, his legacy lives on. On any given day, several dozen of his photos can be found and purchased on-line. Hundreds more can be viewed on various social media sites. And the majority of the approximately 600 images that were left to his heirs have been digitally reproduced and are displayed on-line as well. He is arguably the most prolific Broadway photographer ever. In 1935 Korman claimed to shoot "50,000 gorgeous girls a year."[119] A 1937 article, only halfway through his career, goes so far as to say "he has photographed more than 300,000 women in some 15 years"[120] Lifetime estimates range as high as a half million. Tragically, the vast majority of his work remains lost to time: destroyed or hidden in fading scrapbooks, dusty shoe boxes or a myriad of other places. Still, and in spite of it all, Korman's life and legacy gives him a legitimate claim to the title, "the one big name."[121]

---

a Two sources attribute Pat's death to suicide but the author could not find records to document this.

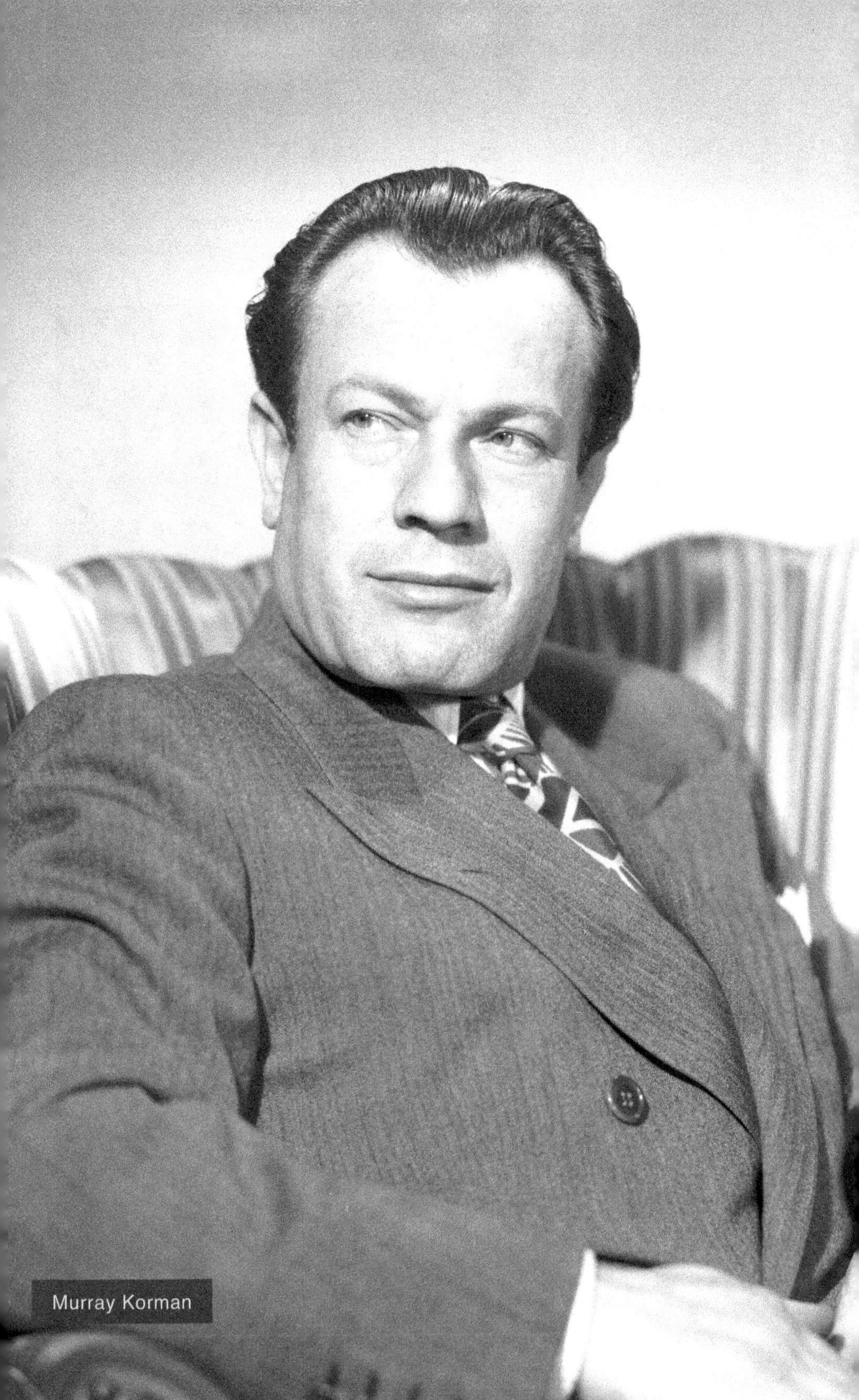
Murray Korman

GALLERY

All photos in this section are provided by the estate of Murray Korman and may not be duplicated in any form.

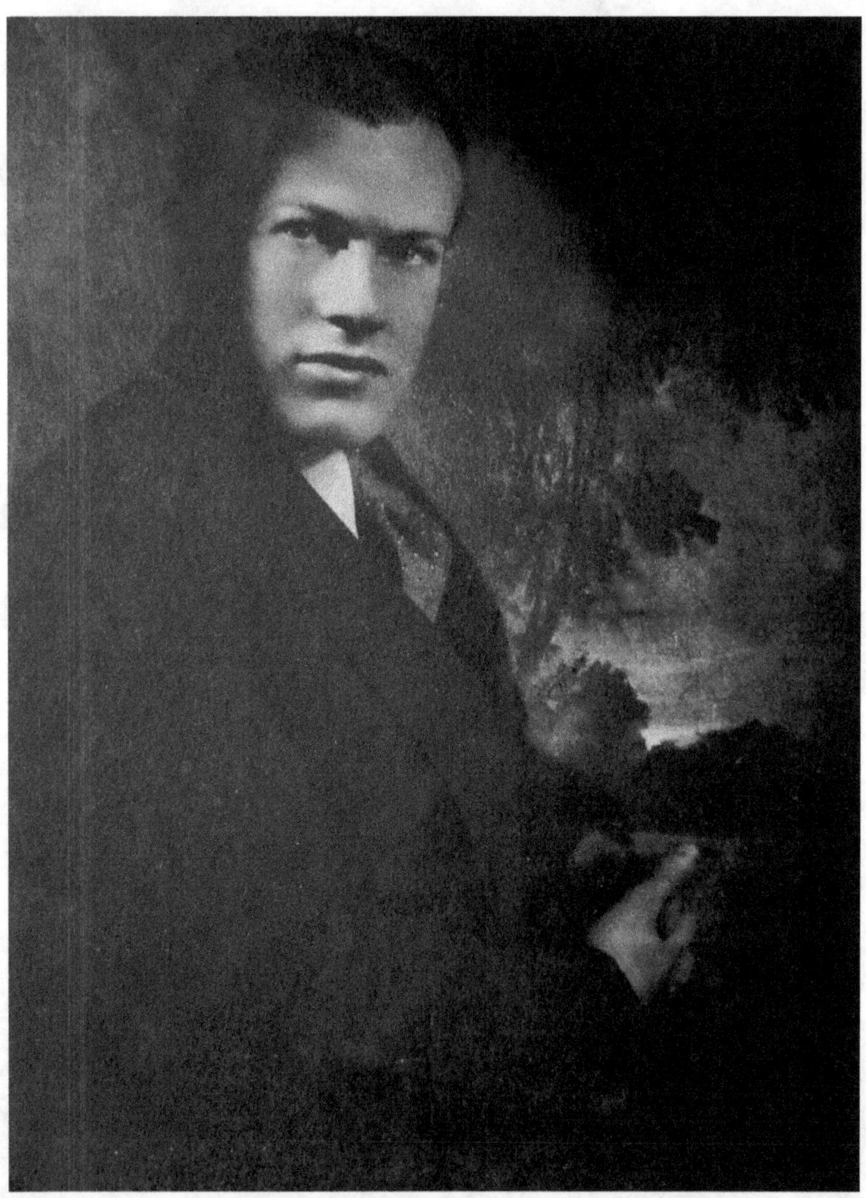

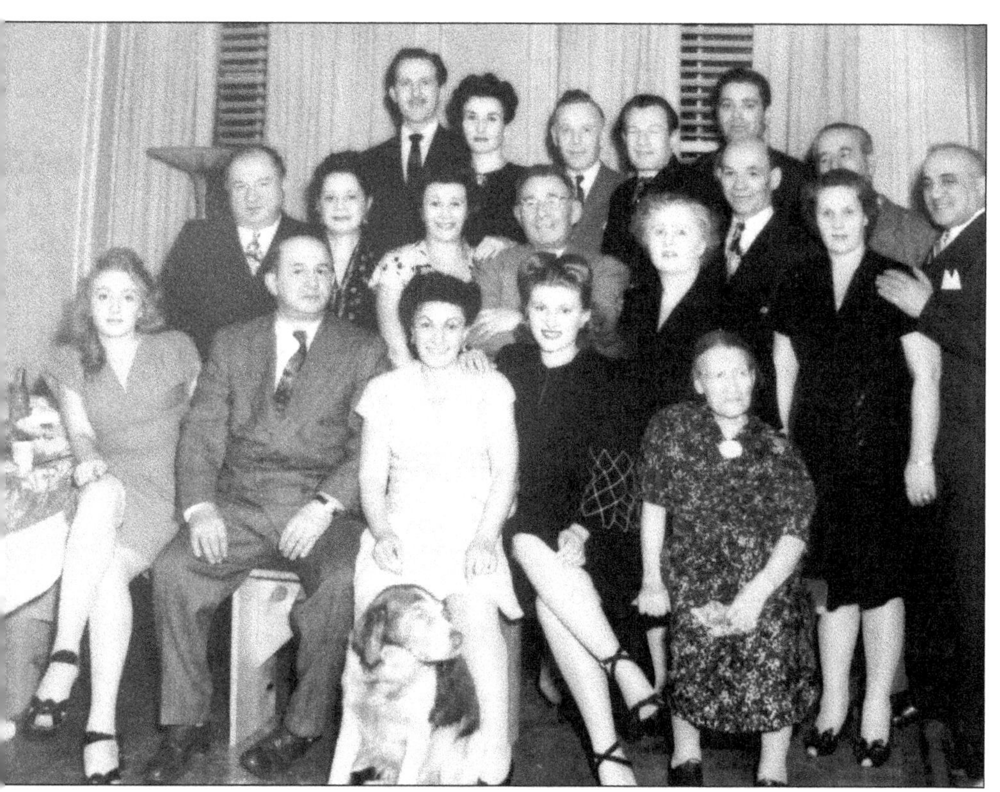

▲ The photo above was taken in 1947 at the 25th wedding anniversary celebration of Jean and Nathan Satro, Murray Korman's sister and brother-in-law, Jean and Nathan are seated on the front row, the second and third from the left. Murray can be seen fourth from the left on the back row. Murray's brother and business partner, Harry, is standing in front and to the left of Murray–the only person in the photo wearing glasses. Murray's two nieces who inherited his estate, Roberta and Sally Satro sit to the left and right of their parents respectively. Murray's step mother, Ida Korman, is seated to the far right on the front row.

◀ The photo on the facing page is a portrait of a young Murray Korman.

The following pages are photos made from negatives that are the property of the Murray Korman's estate. They represent a small sampling of "the Master's" work resurrected in 2013, after more than half a century of storage in a New York City apartment closet. The first three spreads capture Korman at work in his studio with an entourage identified simply as "Earl Lindsays."

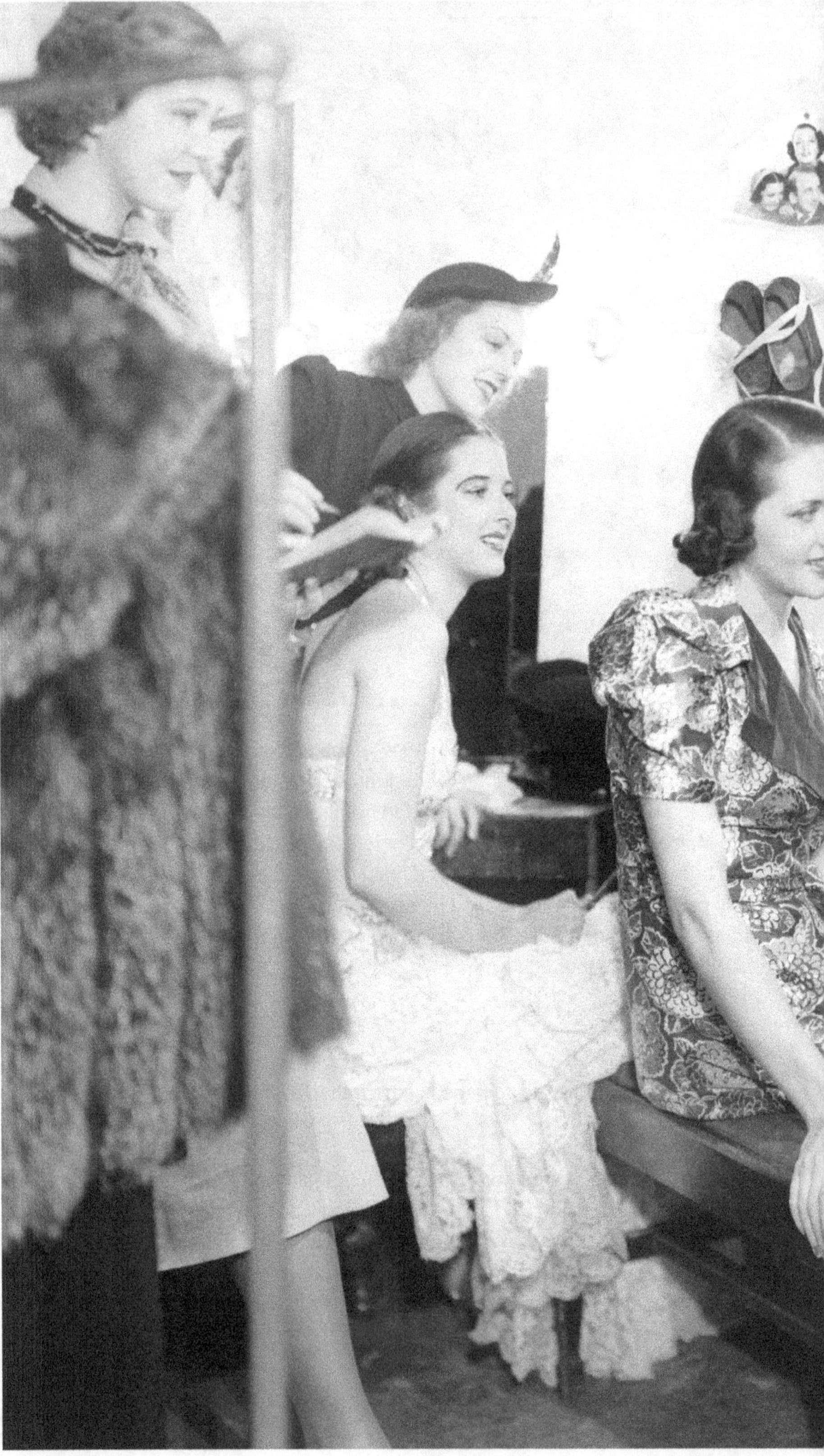

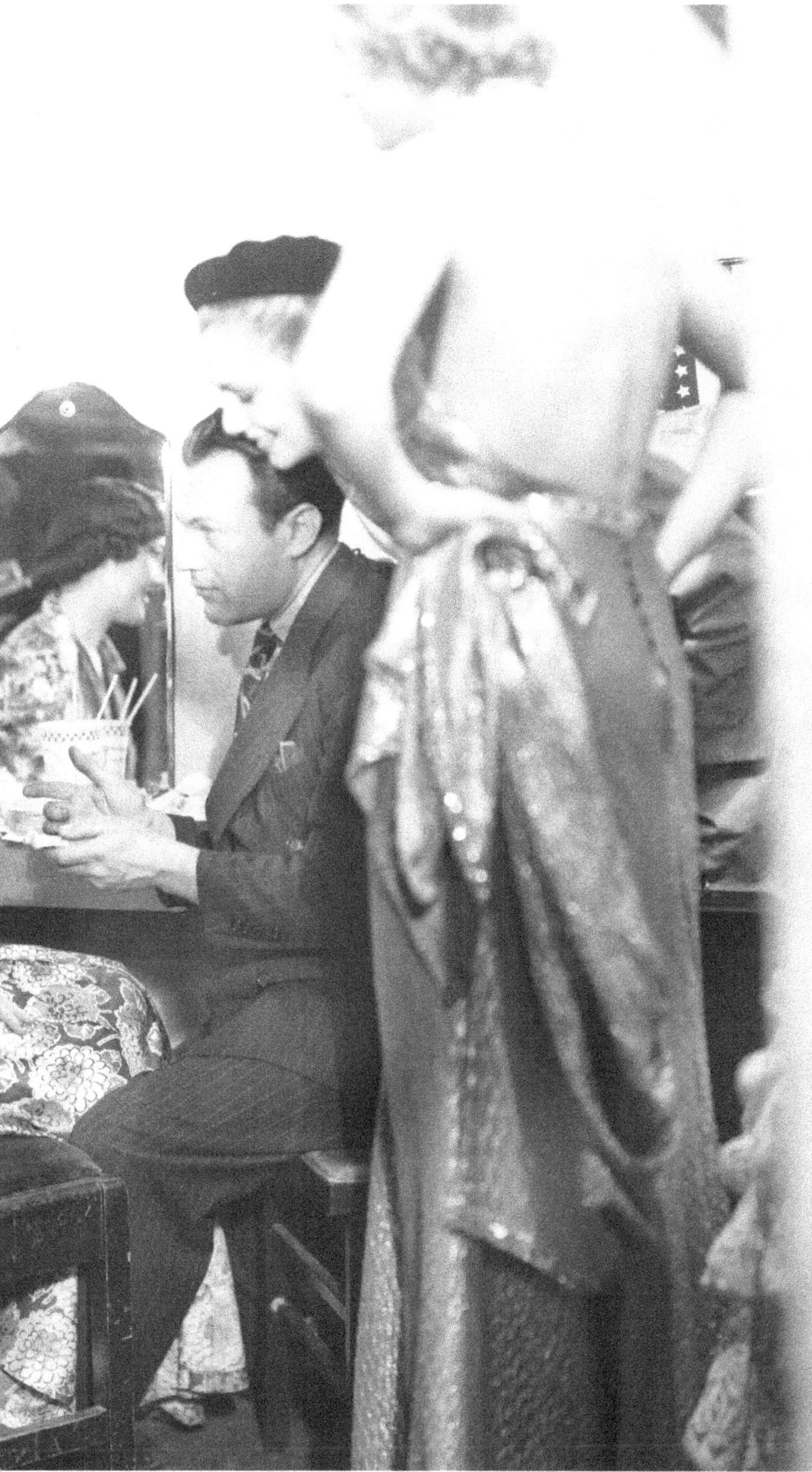

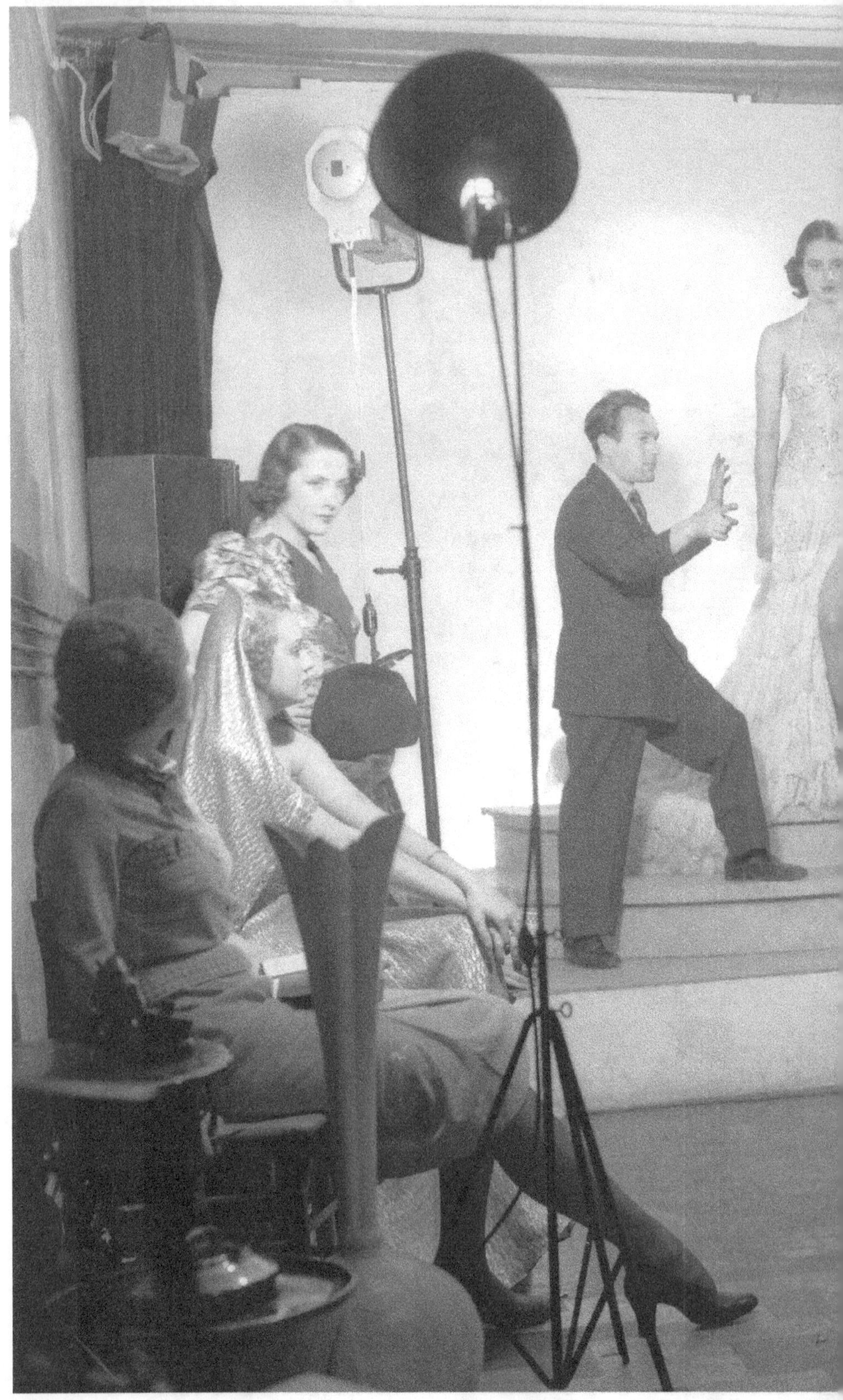

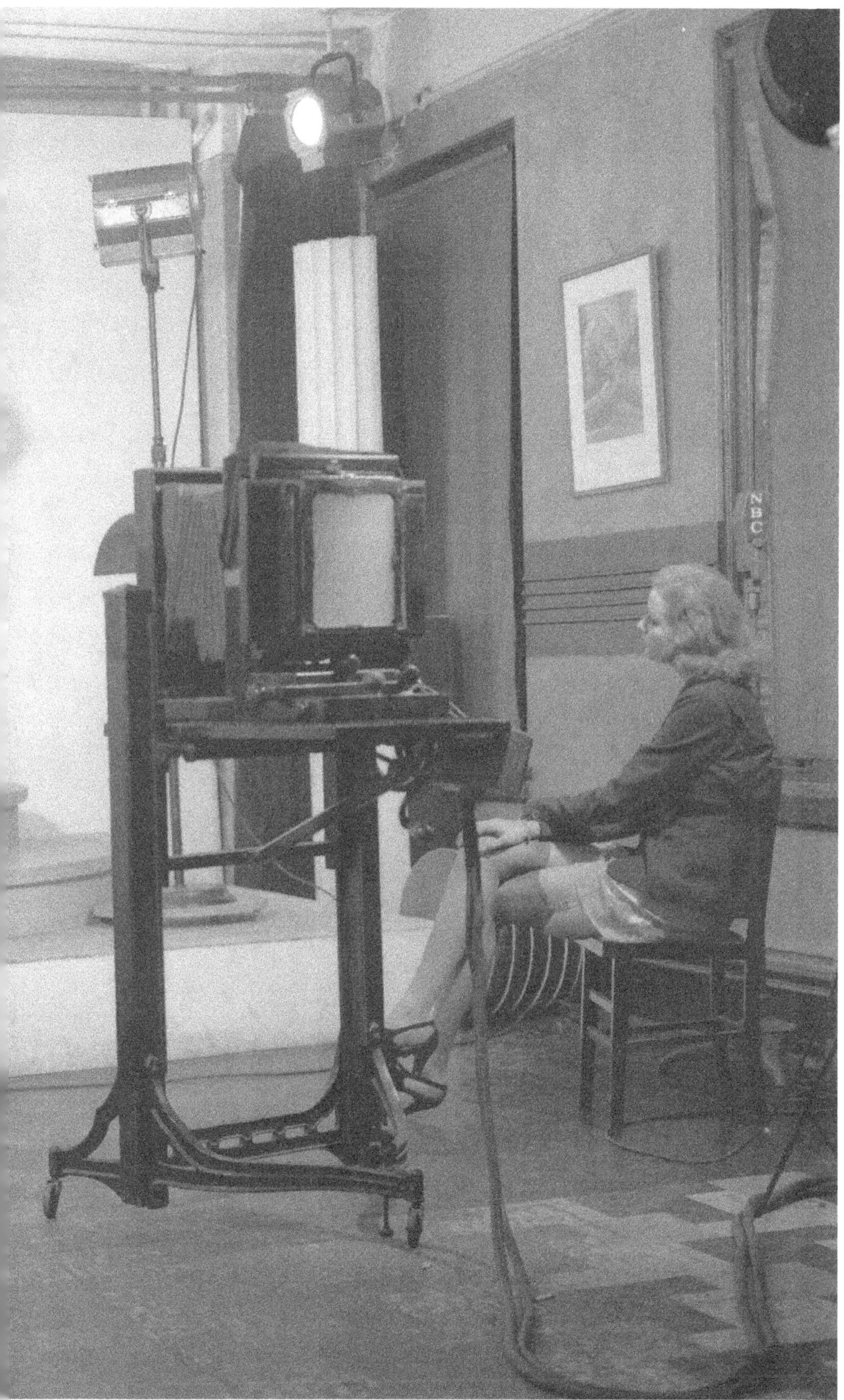
NBC

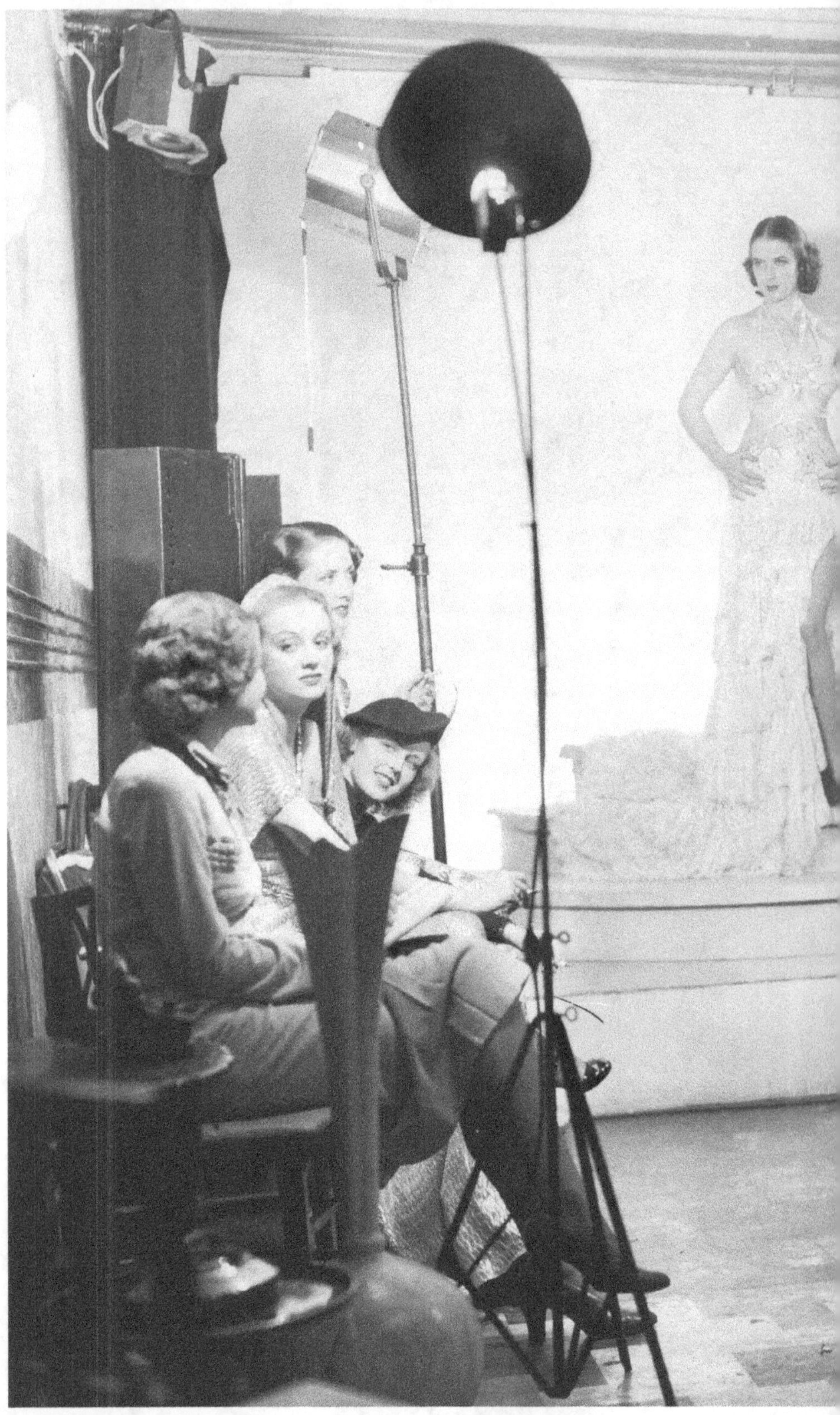

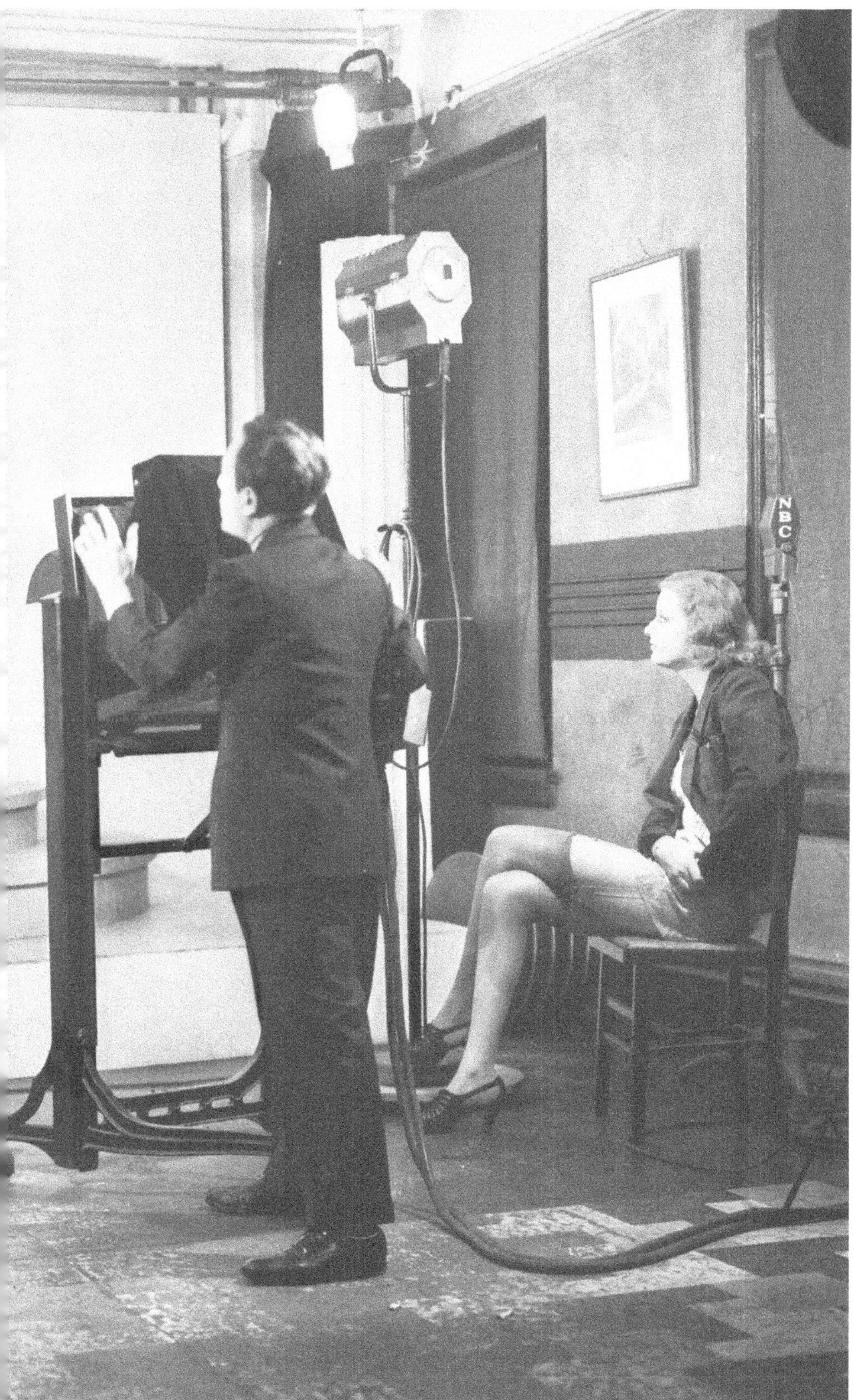
NBC

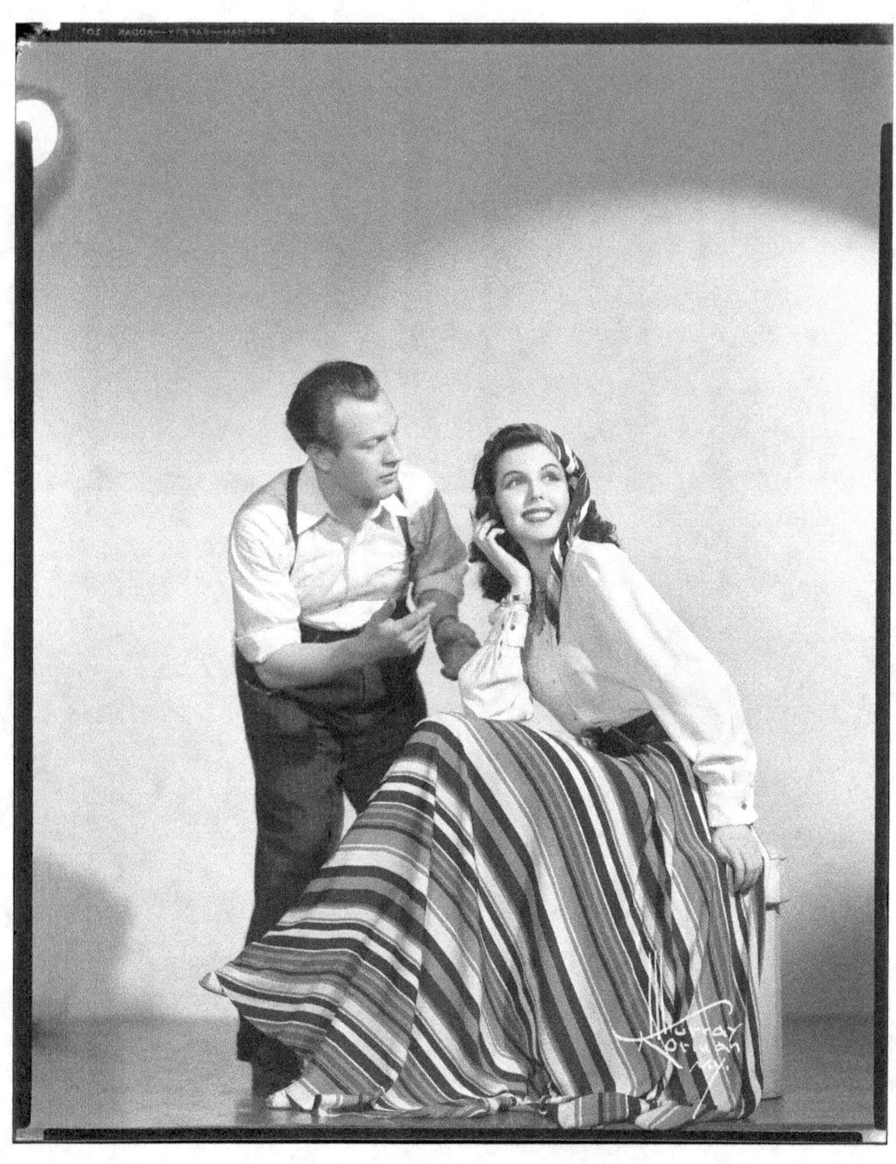

Korman poses Ann Miller.

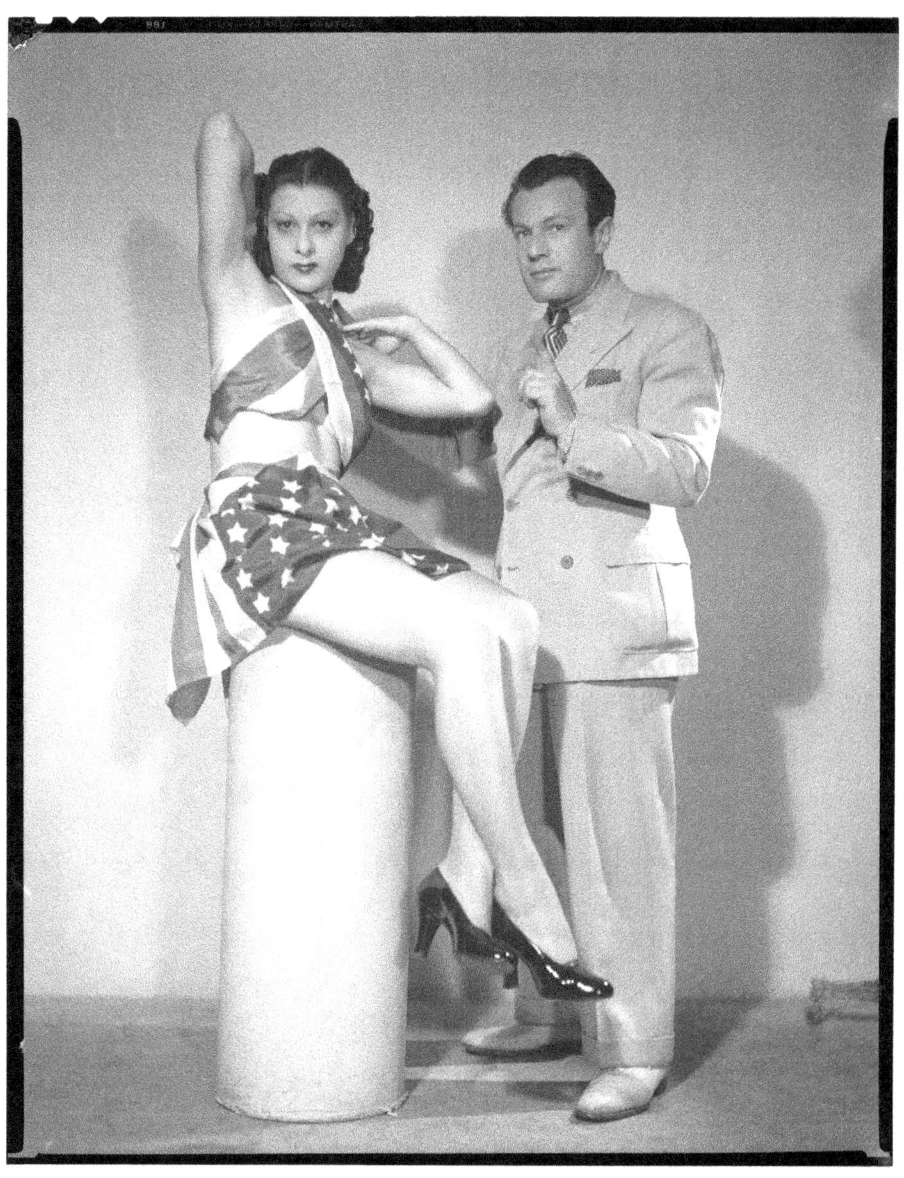

Korman poses with an unidentified model.

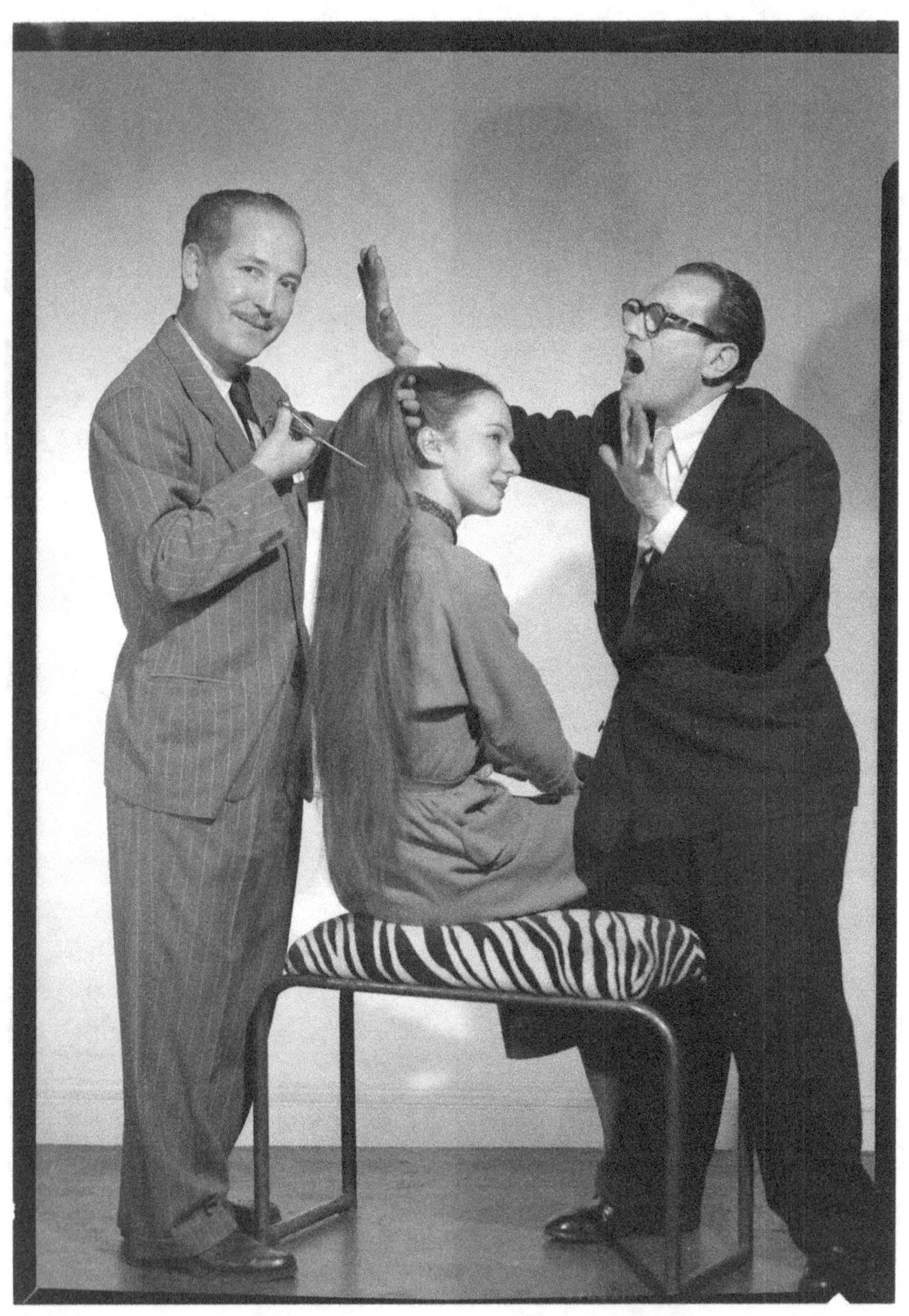

Korman hams it up with unidentified models.

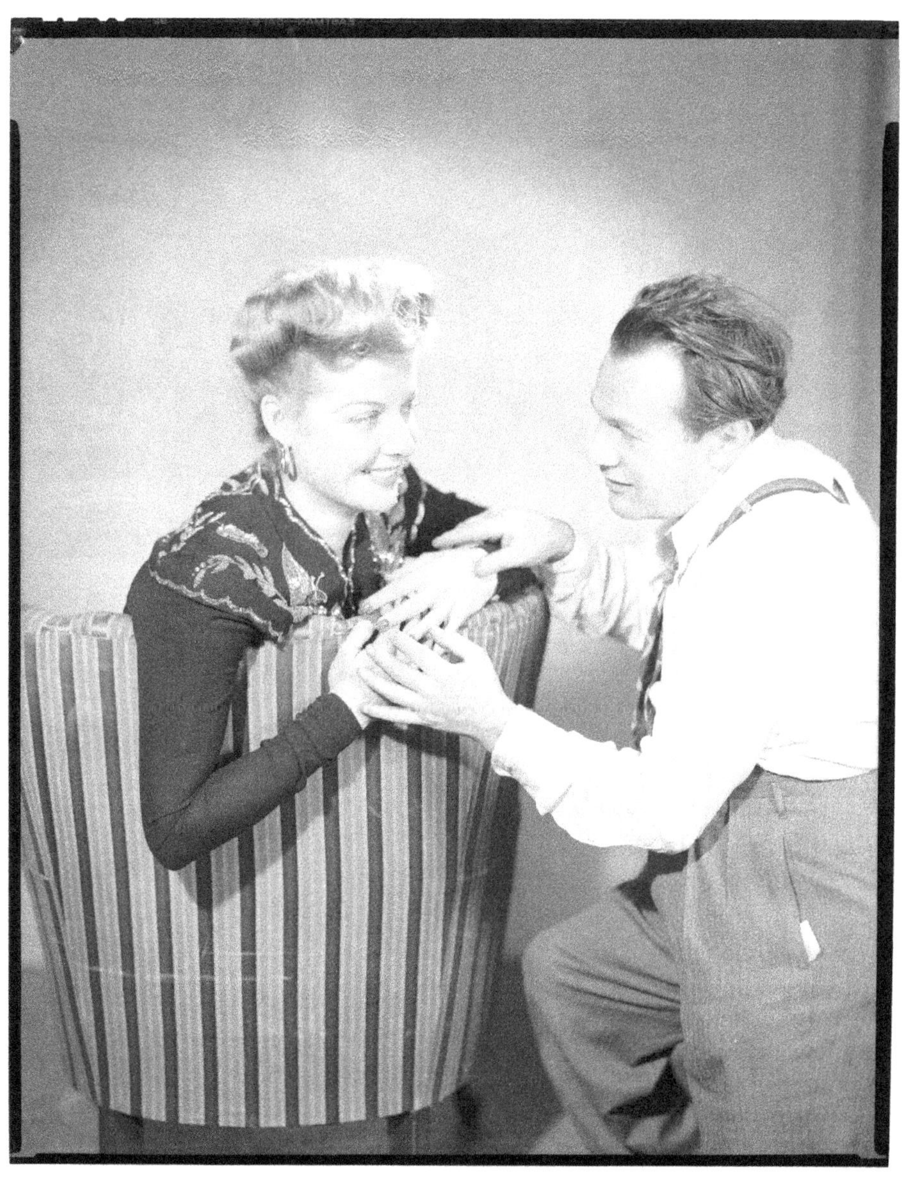

Korman works with an unidentified model.

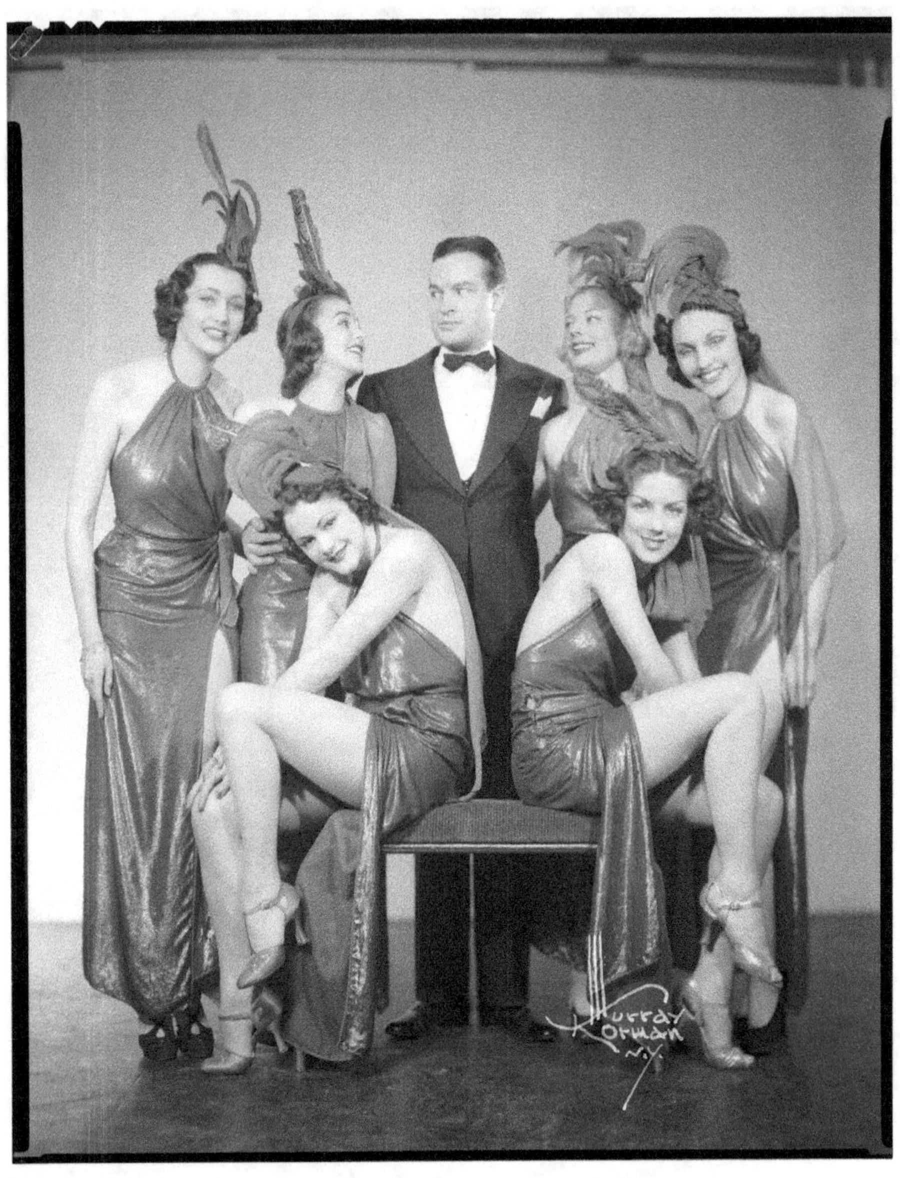

This photo is one of a series featuring Bob Hope and unidentified dancers/ entertainers from the Broadway show, "Red, Hot, and Blue."

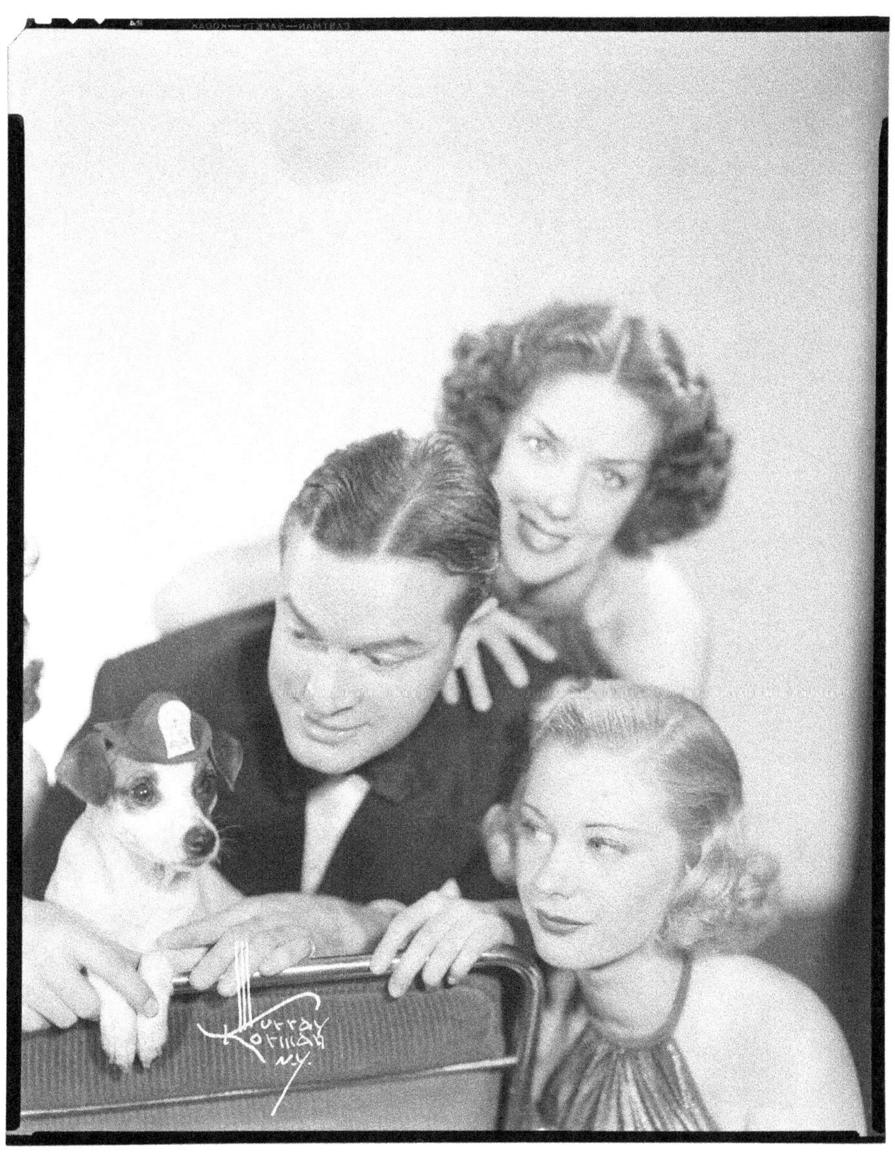

This photo is one of a series featuring Bob Hope and unidentified dancers/ entertainers from the Broadway show, “Red, Hot, and Blue.”

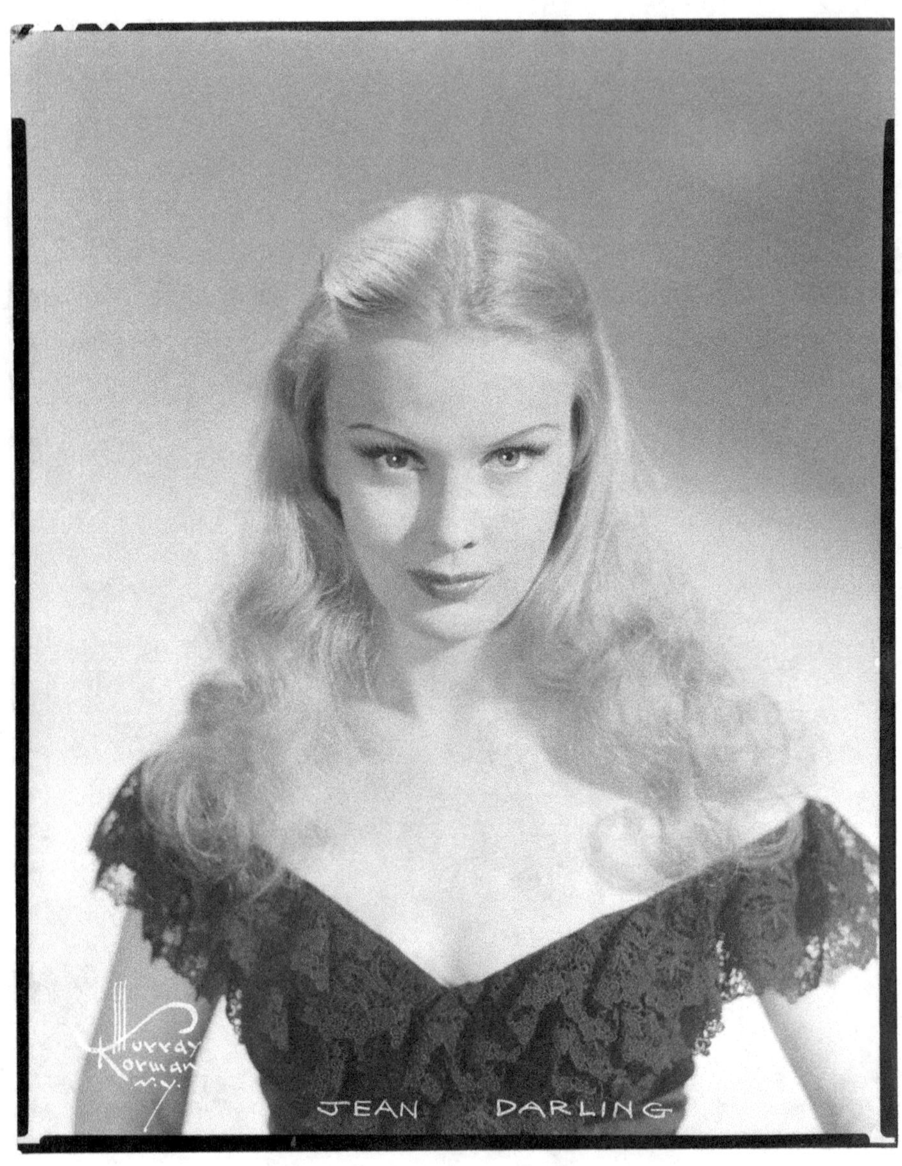

Actress Jean Darling. Jean was one of the original cast of the Little Rascals.

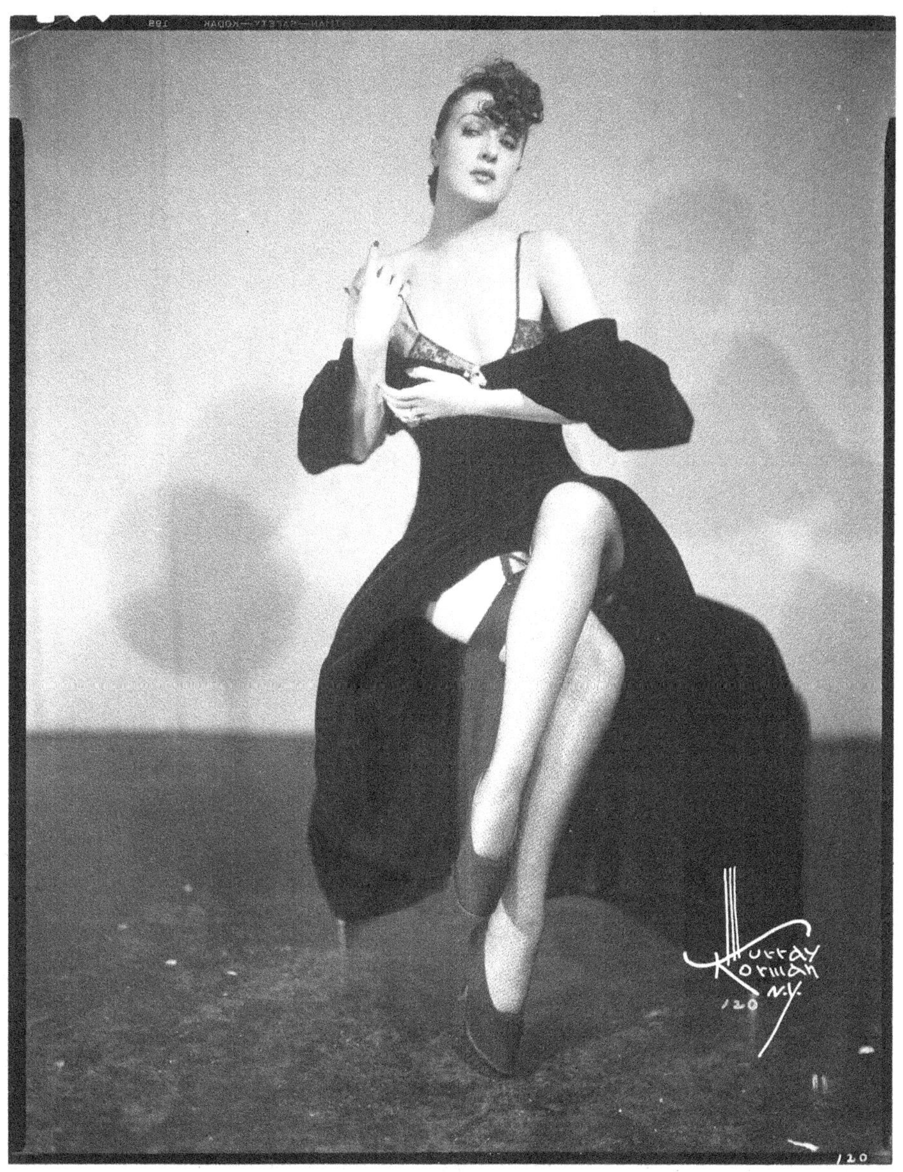

Burlesque dancer, actress, author, and playwright, Gypsy Rose Lee.

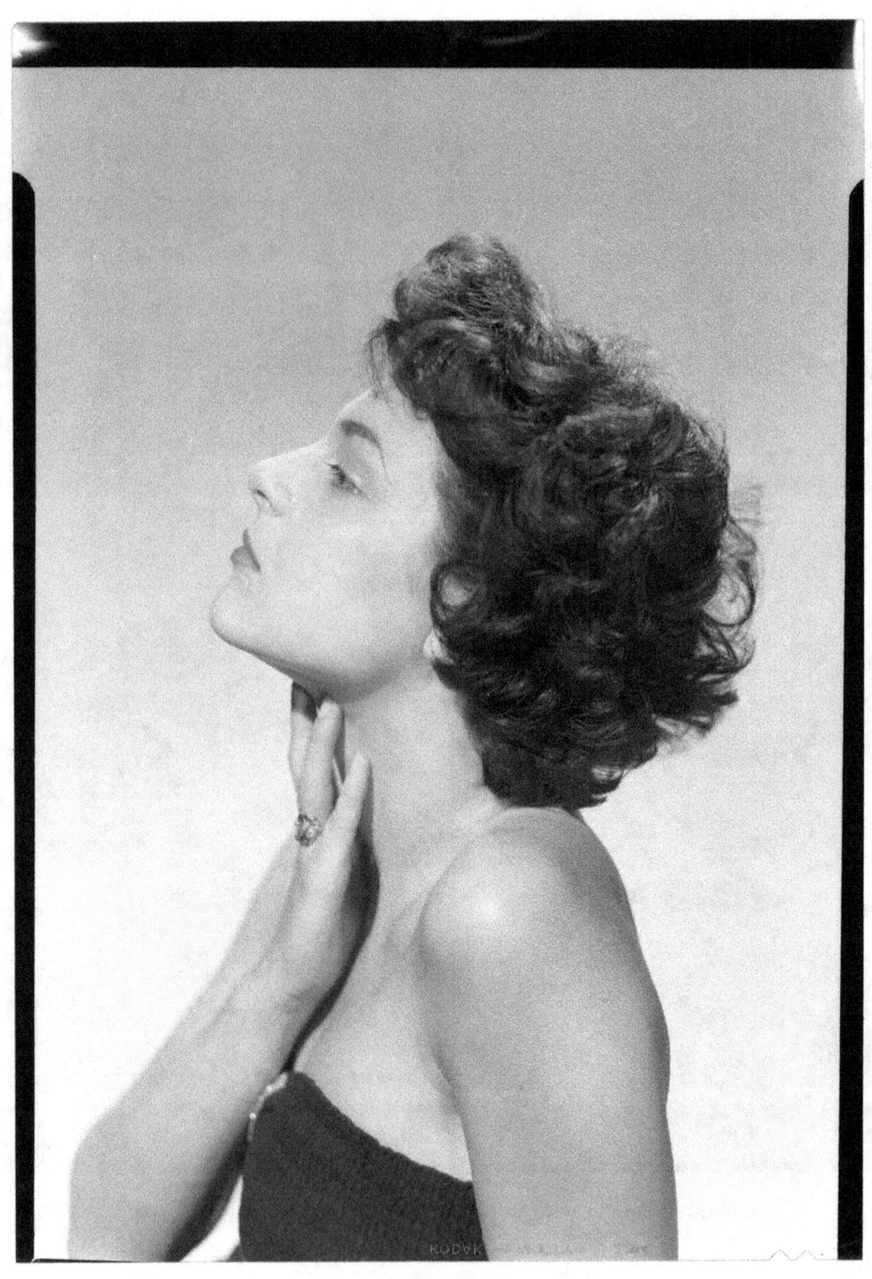

Actress, director, screenwriter and singer, Ann Bancroft.

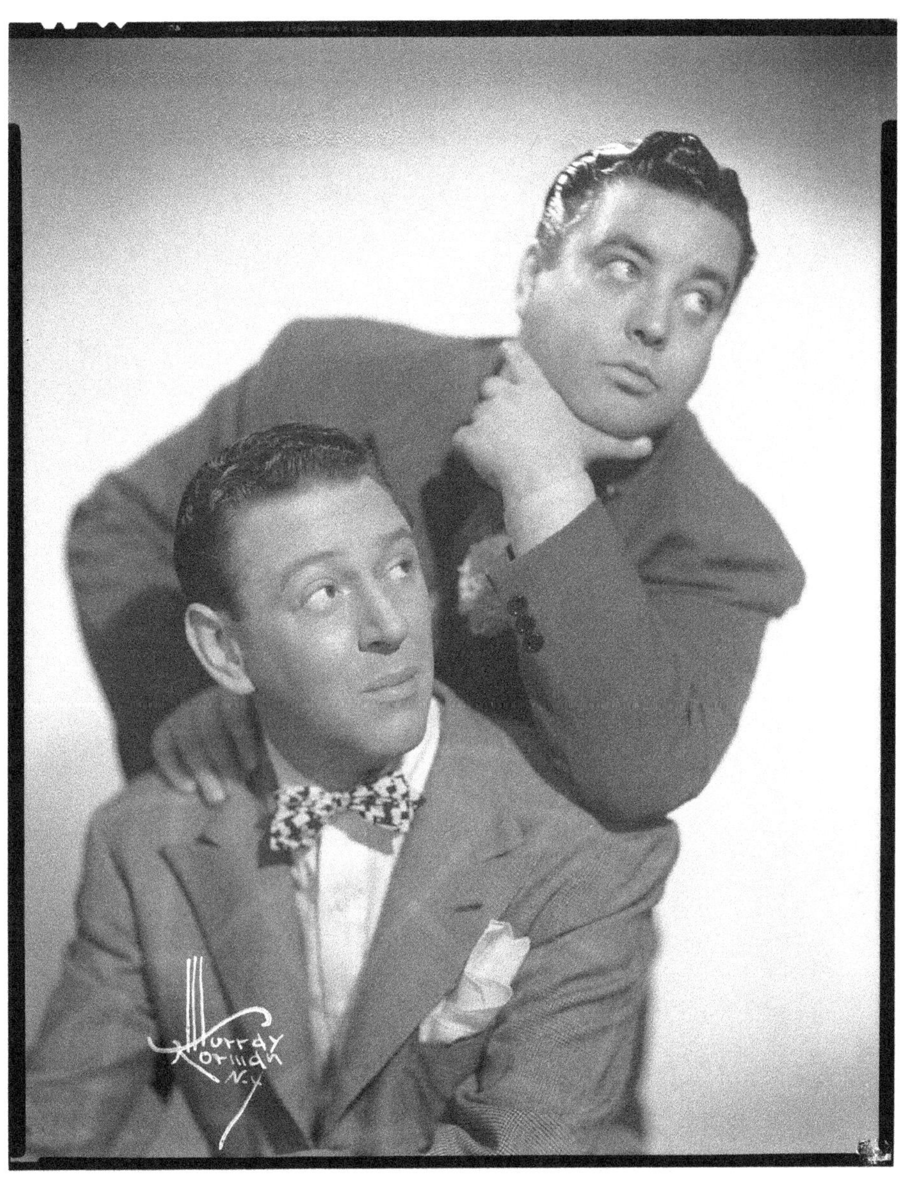

Actor, comedian, writer, composer and conductor,
Jackie Gleason (standing) with fellow comedian Lew Parker.

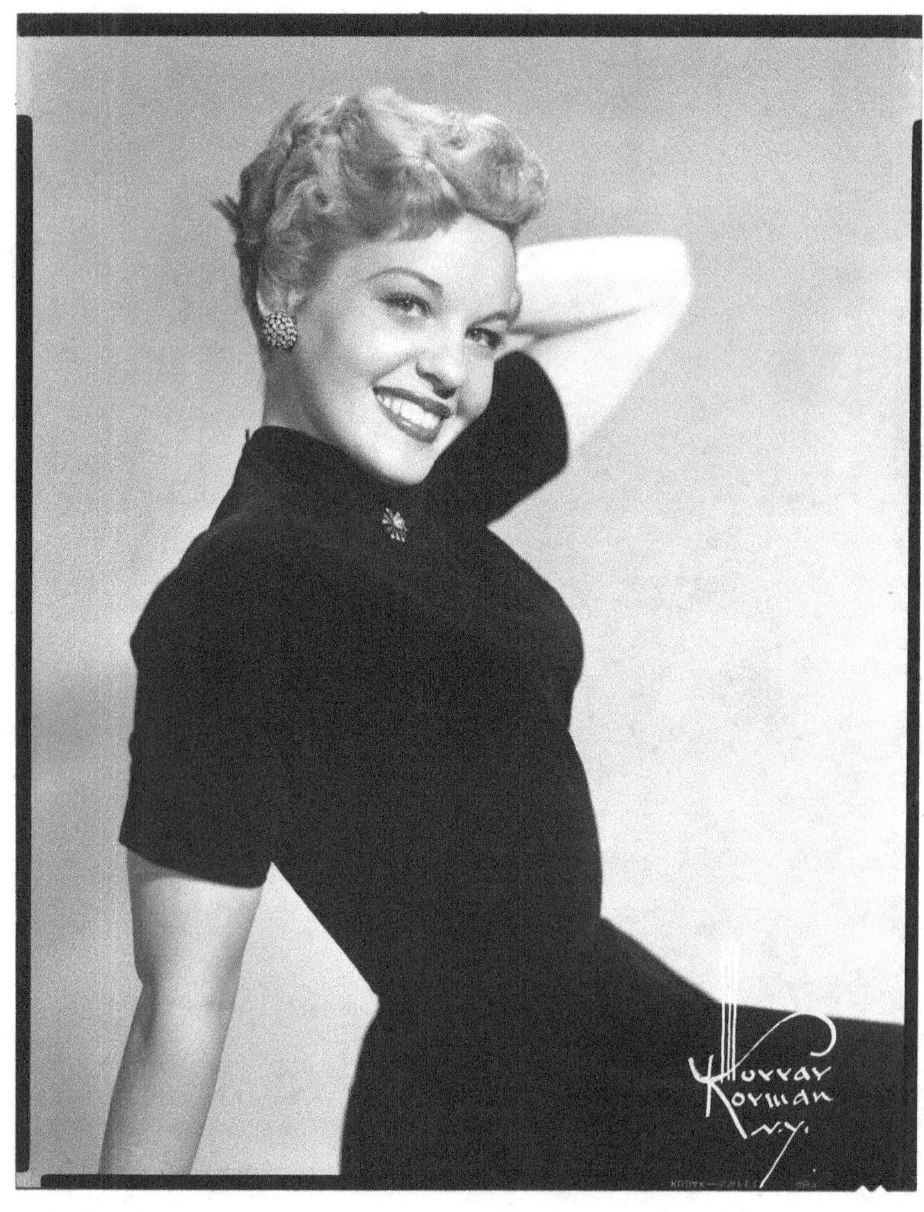

Singer and actress, Jaye P. Morgan. Morgan is well known among a generation as a judge on the 1970s game show, *The Gong Show.*

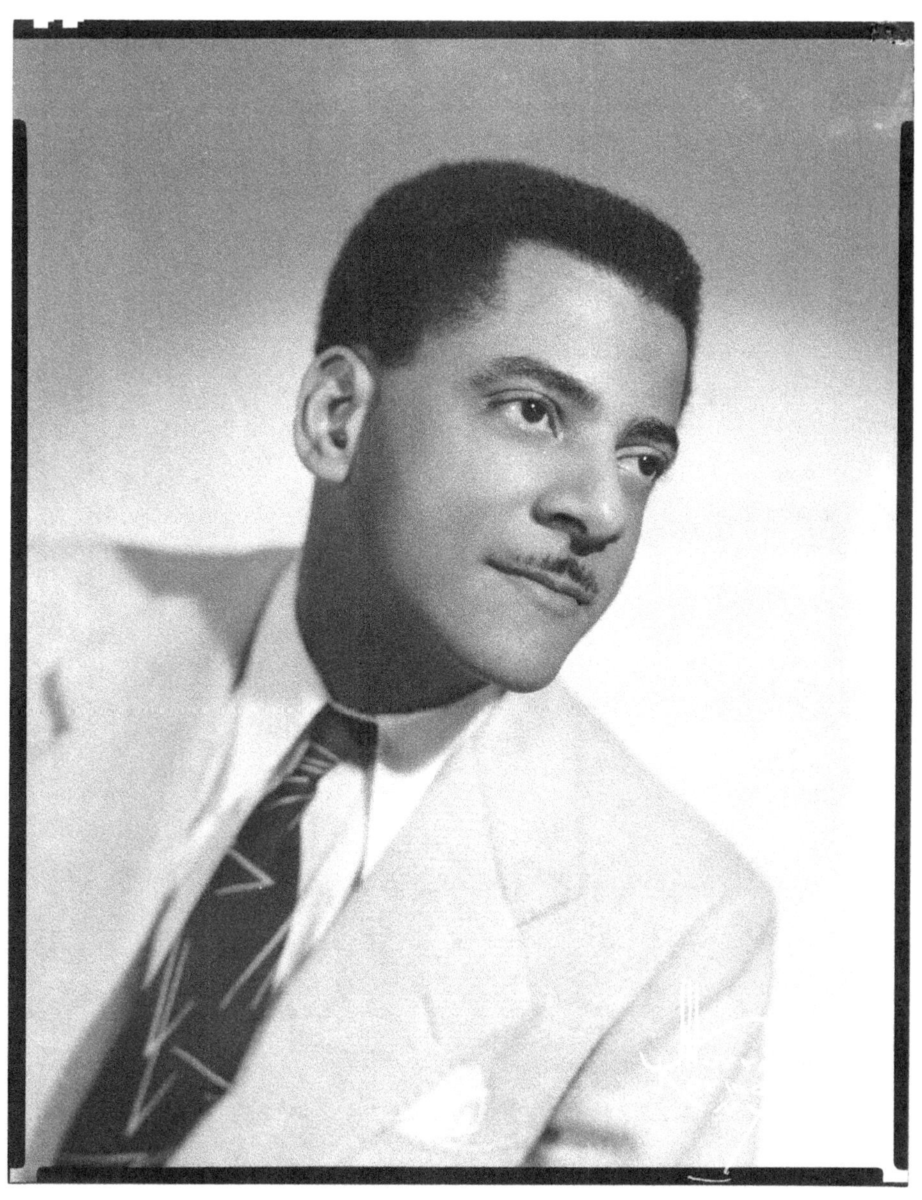

Jazz musician, Teddy Wilson.

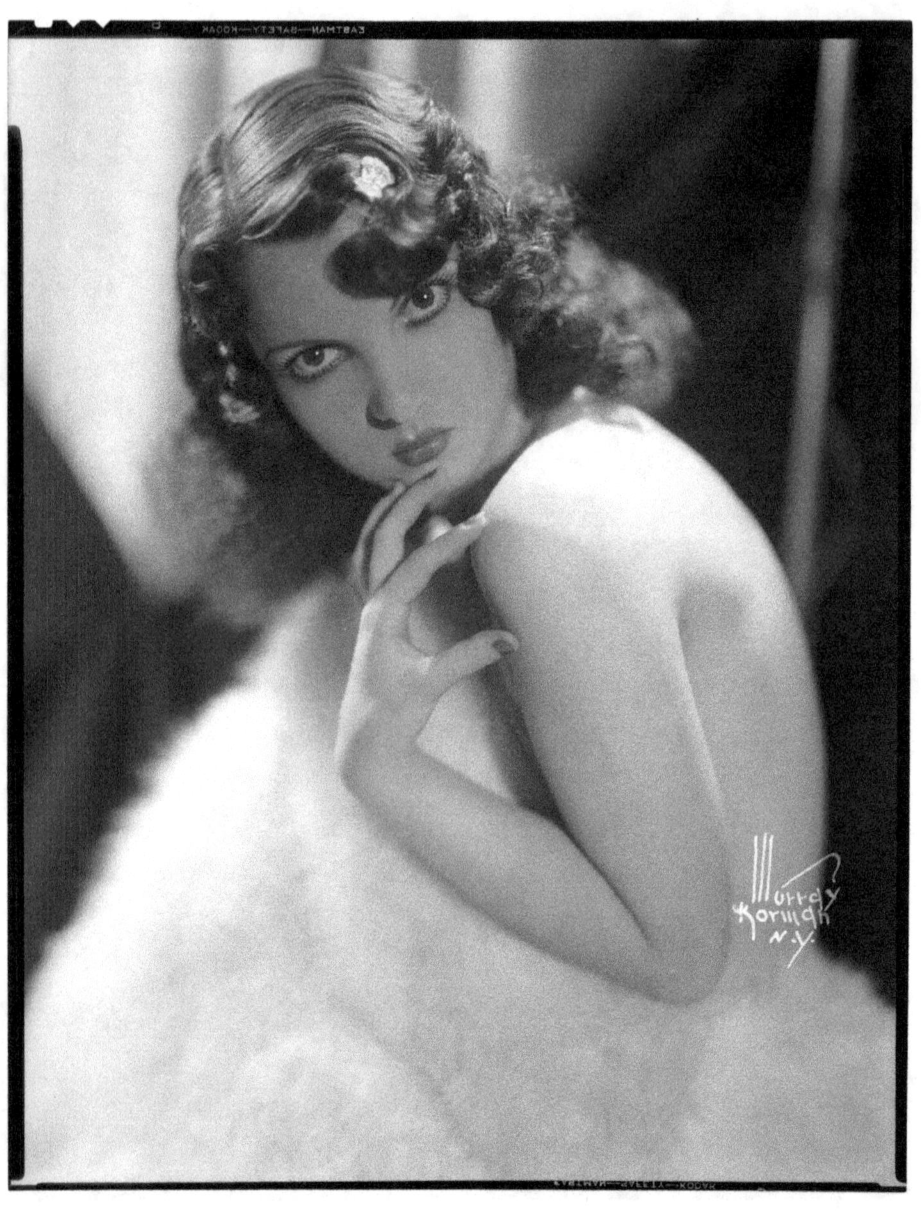

Burlesque dancer Ann Corio.

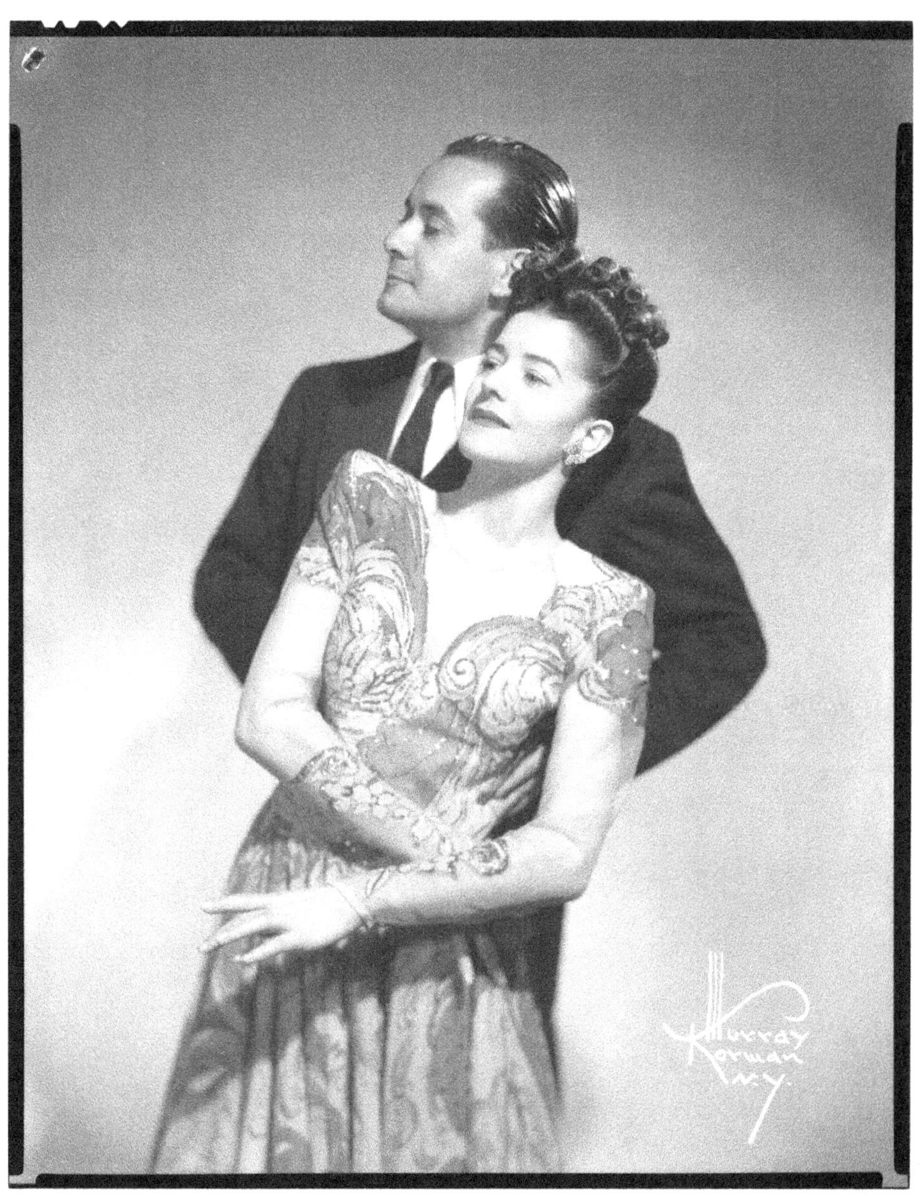

Dancers identified on negative sleeve simply as Jose & Mona.

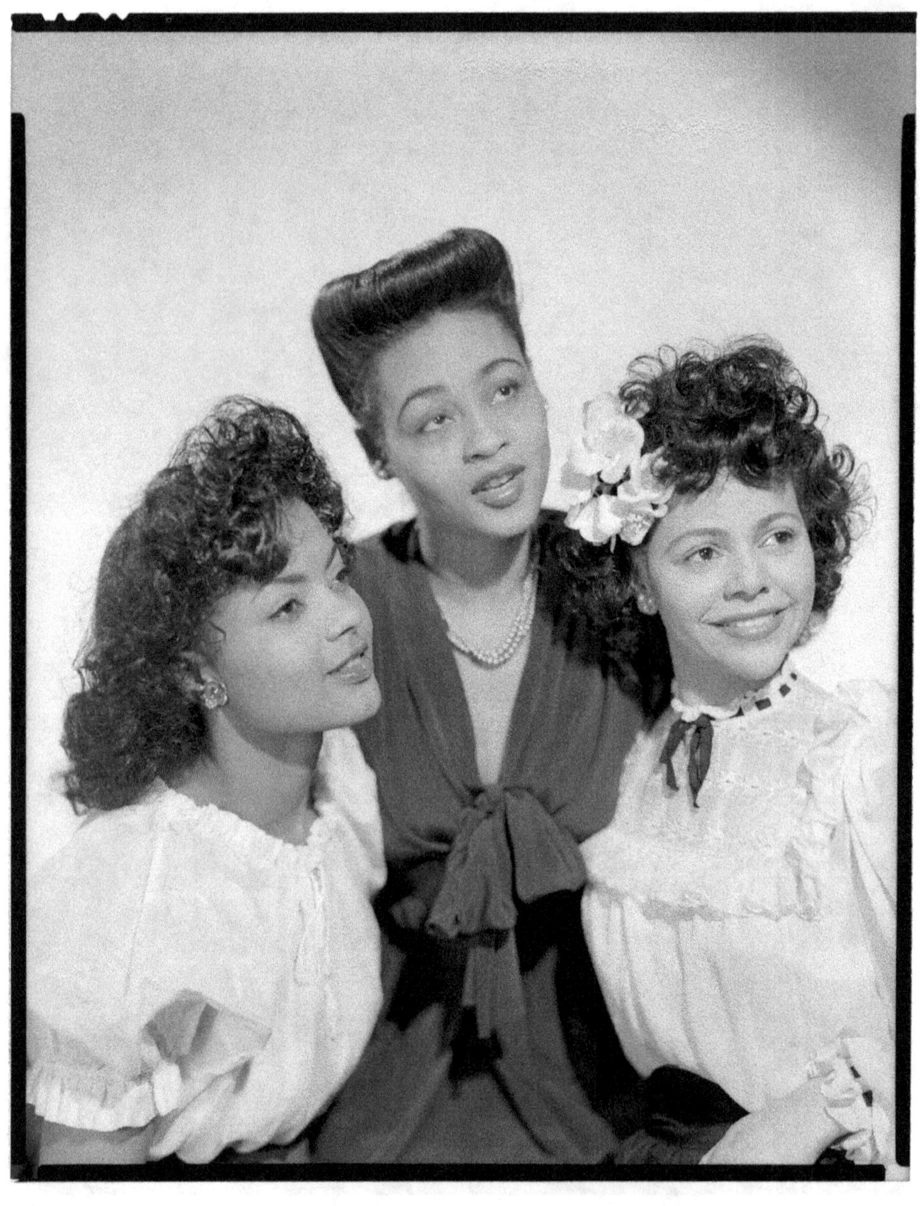

From left to right, Sheila Guyse, Ida James and Thelma Carpenter, all members of the cast of the Broadway play, *Memphis Bound*.

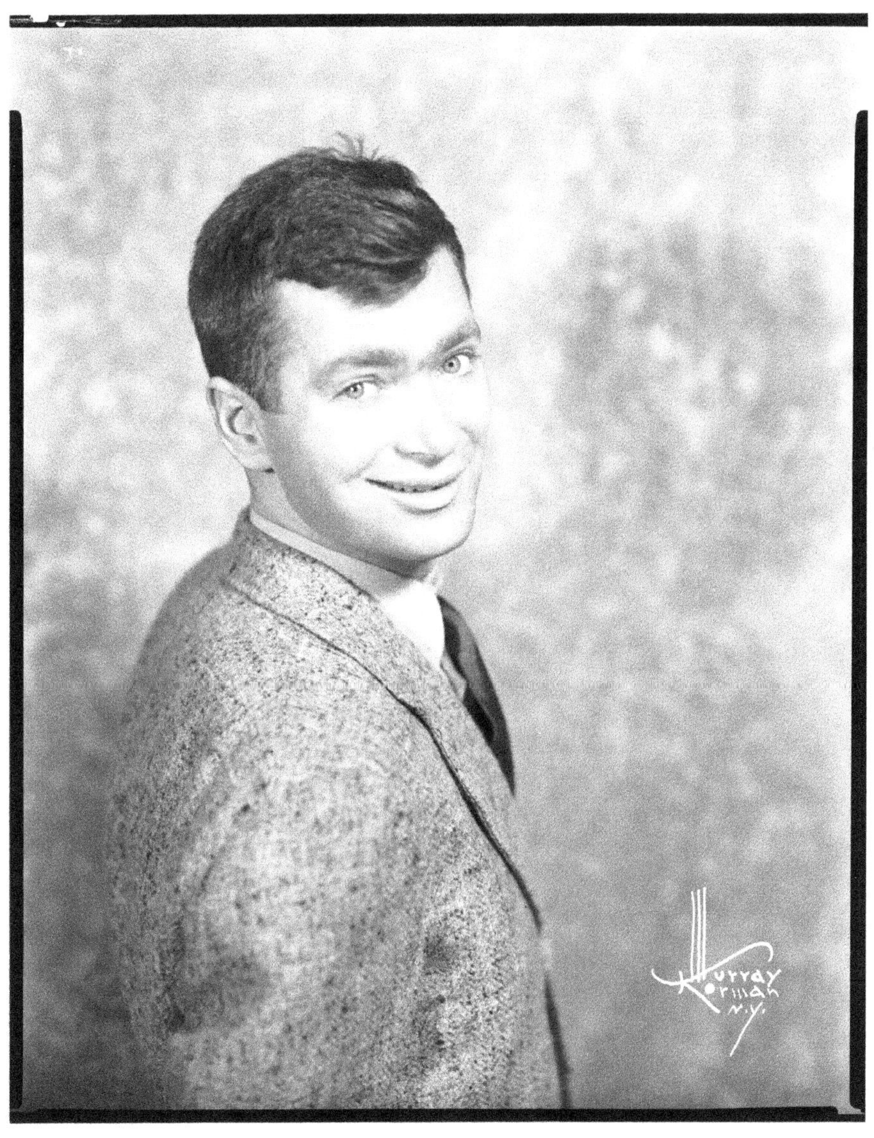

Actor Buddy Ebsen. Ebsen became best known for his role in the sitcom *Beverly Hillbillies.*

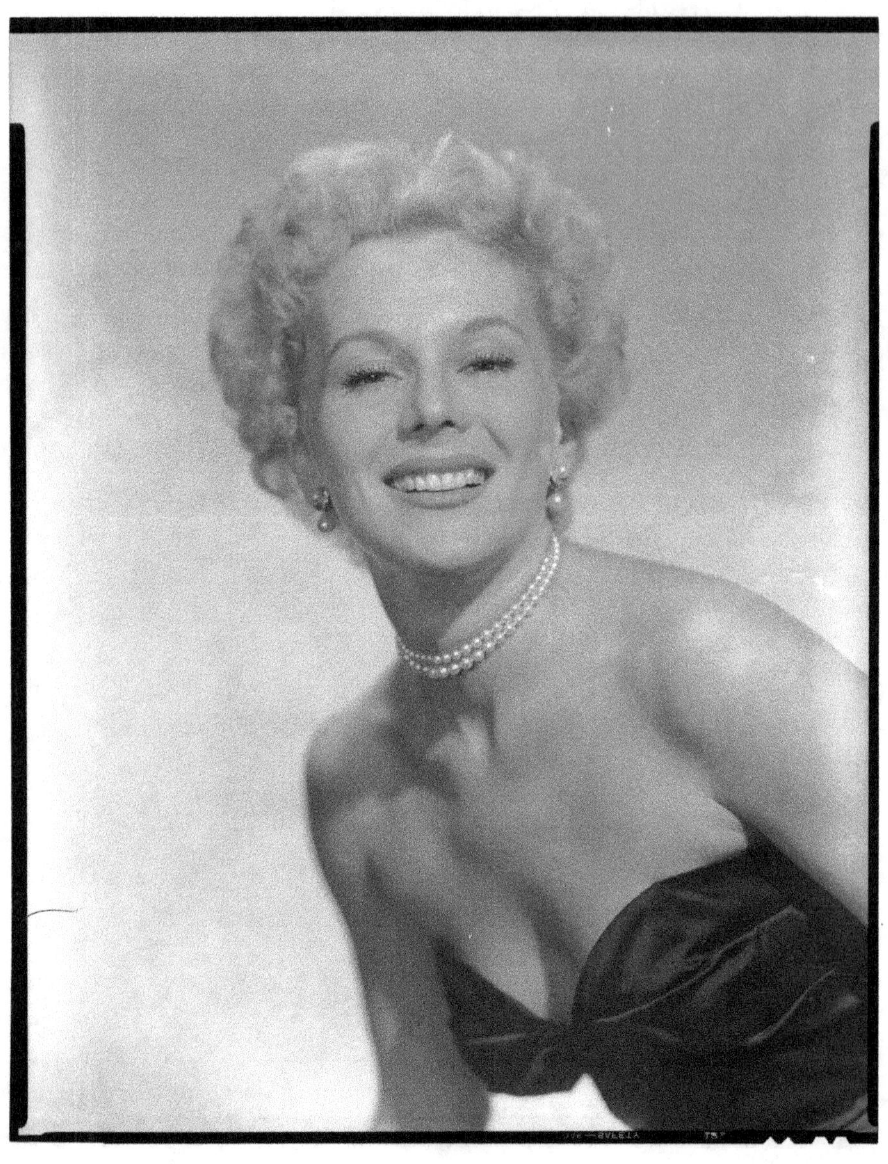

Actress Eva Gabor. Gabor became well known among a generation as Lisa Douglas from the sitcom, *Green Acres.*

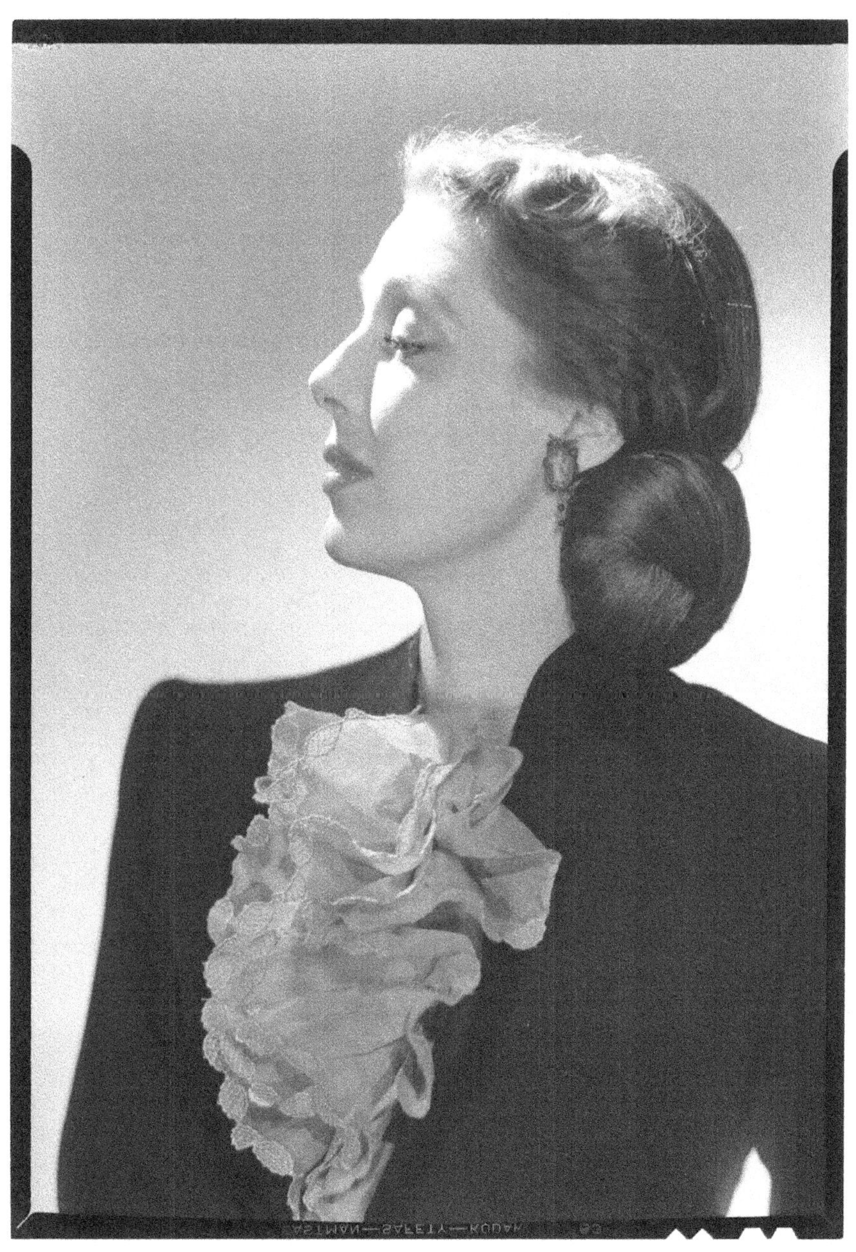

Actress Loretta Young.

ENDNOTES

1 *Arizona Republic*, June 1, 1941

2 *The New Yorker* magazine, October 1942.

3 *American Heritage* on-line, Volume 55, Issue 6. *The Industrial Age 1865 To 1917*, Donald L. Miller, https://www.americanheritage.com/industrial-age-1865-1917

4 Wikipedia on-line biography. en.wikipedia.org/wiki/Murray_Korman

5 *The New Yorker* magazine, October 1942

6 Ibid.

7 Robert Amell, *Manhattan Unlocked* on-line blog. http://manhattanunlocked.blogspot.com/2011/03/story-behind-lower-east-side.html

8 *The New Yorker* magazine, October 1942

9 Collectors Weekly. https://www.collectorsweekly.com/dolls/kewpie

10 Ibid.

11 *The New Yorker* magazine, October 1942

12 Ibid.

13 Christine Trotter, *Murray Korman with Salvador Dalí, Dream of Venus,* Hofstra University Library Special Collections - Weingrow Collection, http://www.hofstra.edu/PDF/lib_sc_weingrow_usrp_trotter.pdf (accessed November 17, 2014).

14 Ibid.

15 *Popular Photography*, Volume 1, No.7, November 1937

16 *The New Yorker* magazine, October 1942.

17 Obituary from unidentified newspaper. Photocopy obtained from Murray Korman's great-niece, Leslie Greaves.

18 *Photo Arts Magazine*, October 1952

19 Dr. David S. Shields, McClintock Professor, University of South Carolina, *Broadway Photographs.* https://broadway.cas.sc.edu/content/murray-korman

20 *The Milwaukee Journal*, December 28, 1938 (The same article appeared in many other publications across the nation throughout the later part of December, 1938.)

21 *The New Yorker* magazine article, October 1942

22 *Popular Photography* magazine, November 1937

23 Laurie Jo Miller Farr, *New York Broadway Theater Facts.* USA Today on-line. https://traveltips.usatoday.com/new-york-broadway-theater-facts-21806.html]

24 History Things, *The History of Broadway.* https://historythings.com/the-history-of-broadway/

25 Kelli Trapnell, *History of NYC Streets: The Great White Way,* Untapped New York. https://untappedcities.com/2012/12/06/history-of-streets-the-great-white-way/

26 Spotlight on Broadway, *Broadway History.* https://www.spotlightonbroadway.com/the-great-white-way-0

27 Great White Way. http://greatwhiteway.com/about.shtml
28 Spotlight on Broadway, *Broadway History.* https://www.spotlightonbroadway.com/the-great-white-way-0
29 *The New Yorker* magazine, October 1942
30 *The Missoulian*, Missoula, Montana. Sunday, Dec 25, 1938 · Page 25
31 *The New Yorker* magazine, October 1942, pg. 24
32 *The Milwaukee Journal*, December 28, 1938
33 *The Brooklyn Daily Eagle*, August 28, 1929
34 *The Daily News,* March 29, 1930.
35 *The Arizona Republic*, June 1, 1941,
36 *The New Yorker* magazine, October 1942
37 Ibid.
38 Ibid.
39 *Delaware County Daily Times,* James Aswell
40 *New York Times* obituary
41 Ibid.
42 *The Milwaukee Journal*, December 28, 1938
43 Ibid.
44 *Popular Photography*, Volumne 1, No.7, November 1937
45 *The Arizona Republic,* June 1, 1948
46 *The Springfield Daily Republican,* June 3, 1941
47 *The New Yorker* magazine, October 1942
48 *Daily News*, December 16, 1948.
49 *The Milwaukee Journal*, December 28, 1938
50 *Popular Photography*, November 1937
51 Obituary from unidentified newspaper. (Photocopy obtained from Murray Korman's great-niece, Leslie Greaves).
52 *The New Yorker* magazine, October 1942.
53 Ibid.
54 *The Milwaukee Journal*, December 28, 1938
55 Wikipedia on-line biography. https://en.wikipedia.org/wiki/Clare_Boothe_Luce
56 *The New Yorker* magazine article, October 1942
57 *The Arizona Republic,* June 1, 1948
58 *The Springfield Daily Republican,* June 3, 1941
59 *The Arizona Republic,* June 1, 1941
60 *The Springfield Daily Republican,* June 3, 1941
61 *The Arizona Republic,* June 1, 1941
62 Paul Yawitz, *A Toast To An Artist*
63 *The Misssoulian,* December 25, 1938

64 *Popular Photography*, Volume 1, No.7, November 1937

65 Paul Yawitz, *A Toast To An Artist*

66 Ibid.

67 *The New Yorker* magazine, October 1942, page 24.

68 *It's on the Cards - The History of Cigarette Cards and Trade Cards,* https://www.londoncigcard.co.uk/cardhistory

69 Ibid..

70 *New York Times*, August 10, 1961

71 Larry J. Hoefling, *Nils Thor Granlund: Show Business Entrepreneur and America's First Radio Star*

72 Ibid.

73 *The Daily News*, May 23, 1930

74 Wikipedia. https://en.wikipedia.org/wiki/Bruno_Bernard

75 Roberta Satro. Phone interview by Clyde Adams, 8/24/18

76 *The Daily News,* Nov. 7, 1942

77 Walter Winchell column, August 4, 1960

78 Wikipedia. https://en.wikipedia.org/wiki/James_J._Kriegsmann

79 James Kriegsmann, Jr. (son of James Kriegsmann.) Phone interview by Clyde Adams, May 1, 2020

80 *Popular Photography,* Volume 1, No. 7., November 1937.

81 *PIC* magazine article, The Cheesecake King, January 1950, page20.

82 Hofstra University Library Special Collections - Weingrow Collection, http://www.hofstra.

83 Christine Trotter, *Murray Korman with Salvador Dalí, Dream of Venus,* Hofstra University Library Special Collections - Weingrow Collection, http://www.hofstra.edu/PDF/lib_sc_weingrow_usrp_trotter.pdf (accessed November 17, 2014).

84 *Pampa Daily News*, April 20, 1937

85 *Bradford Evening Star*, New Brunswick, New Jersey.

86 *Lee Mortimer.* https://en.wikipedia.org/wiki/Lee_Mortimer.

87 Ibid.

88 Dr. David S. Shields, McClintock Professor, University of South Carolina, *Broadway Photographs.* https://broadway.cas.sc.edu/content/murray-korman

89 Wikipedia. https://en.wikipedia.org/wiki/1939_New_York_World%27s_Fair

90 *The Monroe Morning World Sun,* January 10, 1937

91 Dorothy Kilgallen's *Voice of Broadway* column

92 *The New Yorker* article, October 1942, page 22

93 Roberta Satro. Phone interview by Clyde Adams, October 2013

94 *Popular Photography*, Volume 1, No.7, November 1937

95 Roberta Satro. Phone interview by Clyde Adams, October 20133

96 *Wilkes-Barre Times Leader*

97 Roberta Satro. Phone interview by Clyde Adams, October 2013

98 *The Daily News,* November 28, 1944

99 Wikipedia. https://en.wikipedia.org/wiki/Glad_To_See_You

100 *The Philadelphia Inquirer,* December 31, 1944

101 *Shamokin News-Dispatch*, Shamokin, Pennsylvania.· Mon, Jul 16, 1945 · Page 4

102 Wikipedia. https://en.wikipedia.org/wiki/Errol_Flynn

103 *The Morning Herald,* July 12, 1954

104 *Wilkes Barre Times Leader, The Evening News,* December 29, 1953

105 Obituary from unidentified newspaper. (Photocopy obtained from Murray Korman's great-niece, Leslie Greaves).

106 *Anniston Star*, Anniston, Alabama, May 2, 1950,

107 Ed Sullivan, *Little Old New York* column, November 6, 1950

. Papermag.com

108 Obituary from unidentified newspaper. (Photocopy obtained from Murray Korman's great-niece, Leslie Greaves).

109 Mitch Ross (son of Gil Ross.) Phone interview by Clyde Adams, April 1, 2020.

110 *The Bygone Era of the Jewish Catskills Resorts*, Sheldon Kirshner, https://blogs.timesofisrael.com/the-bygone-era-of-the-jewish-catskills-resorts/

111 Ibid.

112 *Pottsville Republican*, July 29, 1958.jpg

113 Dr. David S. Shields, McClintock Professor, University of South Carolina, *Broadway Photographs.* https://broadway.cas.sc.edu/content/herbert-mitchell

114 *The Star Press,* November 29, 1960

115 Earl Wilson's *It Happened Last Night* newspaper column, August 16, 1961

116 *Daily News* (New York, New York). Jan 23, 1961.

117 Roberta Satro. Phone interview by Clyde Adams, October 2013

118 Ibid.

119 *Star Tribune Sun*, February 24, 1935

120 *Pampa Daily News*, April 20, 1937

121 *The New Yorker* magazine, October 1942.

PHOTO CREDITS

Pg. 10	Murray Korman. Scanned from Korman's original negative, property of Murray Korman's estate.
Pg. 16	Soloman Korman and family, property of Murray Korman's estate.
Pg. 22	Kewpie doll, used by permission from Mike and Sammie Slone.
Pg. 25	Illustration of for The Balloon Hoax article in *Aviation Stories and Mechanics* magazine. Magazine property of Clyde Adams.
Pg. 26	Cast of dancers from Hollywood Restaurant. Scanned from Korman's original negative, property of Murray Korman's estate.
Pg. 30-31	Murray Korman sketches, scanned from the original negative. Scanned from Korman's original negative, property of Murray Korman's estate.
Pg. 32	One in a series inherited by Korman's heirs. The only identification, handwritten on the envelope that contained the negatives reads "Earl Lindsay girls." Scanned from Korman's original negative, property of Murray Korman's estate.
Pg. 35	Murray Korman shooting an ad for Piels Beer with unidentified model. Scanned from Korman's original negative, property of Murray Korman's estate.
Pg. 36	Murray Korman with unidentified Miss America pageant entourage. Scanned from Korman's original negative, property of Murray Korman's estate.
Pg. 44	Murray Korman covered with a collection of his photos. Korman used this image for publicity pieces. Scanned from Korman's original negative, property of Murray Korman's estate.
Pg. 51	James Kriegsmann. Courtesy James Kriegsmann, Jr.
Pg. 55	Murray Korman sketching actress Lupe Velez. Property of Clyde Adams
Pg. 56	Murray Korman with actress Joan Newton. Scanned from Korman's original negative, property of Murray Korman's estate.
Pg. 58	Lee Mortimer. Scanned from Korman's original negative, property of Murray Korman's heirs.
Pg. 60	Magazine covers highlighting Murray Korman photography. Magazines property of Clyde Adams.
Pg. 62	The Hollywood Restaurant. Photo by George Mann. Used with permission of his estate, Brad Smith and Dianne Woods.
Pg. 67	Murray Korman confronts Salvador Dali with interpreter Julien Levy. Library of Congress, Prints & Photographs Division, Reproduction number e.g., LC-USZ62-123456.
Pg. 68	Murray Korman with Pat Farrell. Scanned from Korman's original

	negative property of Murray Korman's estate.
Pg. 72	Murray Korman and Pat Farrell at their wedding reception, Cafe Zanzibar. Public domain.
Pg. 76	Pat Farrell. Scanned from Korman's original negative, property of Murray Korman's estate.
Pg. 80	Murray Korman in his studio. Scanned from Korman's original negative, property of Murray Korman's estate.
Pg. 84	Gil Ross. Courtesy of Mitch Ross.
Pg. 87 & 88	Murray Korman's iconic signature. Courtesy of Murray Korman heirs.
Pg. 91	Murray Korman portrait. Scanned from Korman's original negative, property of Murray Korman's estate.
Pg. 92	Murray Korman portrait. Property of the Satro family collection. Used with permission.
Pg. 93	Anniversary party for Nathan and Jean Korman Satro, 1947. Property of the Satro family. Used with permission.
Pg. 94-117	See photo captions for descriptions. Scanned from Korman's original negatives, property of Murray Korman's estate.

FURTHER RESOURCES

To view a more extensive collection of Murray Korman's work, please visit murraykorman.com. To purchase a coffee-table quality book that features some of the best of his work go to blurb.com/b/10273435-murray-korman-photography.

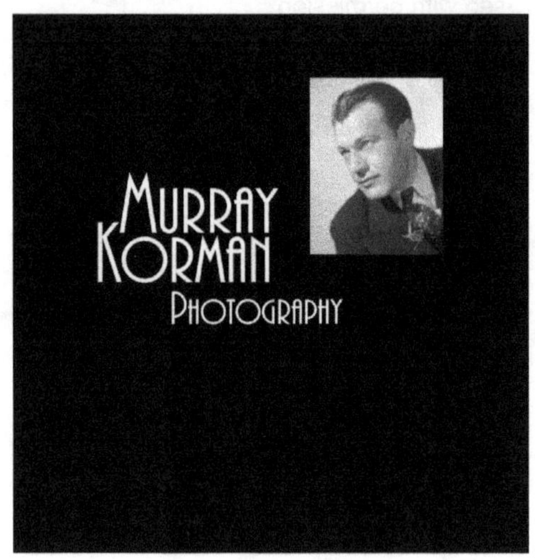

www.ingramcontent.com/pod-product-compliance
Lightning Source LLC
LaVergne TN
LVHW020641100826
845148LV00012B/2291

* 9 7 8 1 7 3 5 1 4 9 4 0 0 *